YOUR KNOWLEDGE HAS VALUE

- We will publish your bachelor's and
  master's thesis, essays and papers

- Your own eBook and book -
  sold worldwide in all relevant shops

- Earn money with each sale

Upload your text at www.GRIN.com
and publish for free

Bibliographic information published by the German National Library:

The German National Library lists this publication in the National Bibliography; detailed bibliographic data are available on the Internet at http://dnb.dnb.de .

Imprint:

Copyright © 2016 GRIN Verlag, Open Publishing GmbH
Print and binding: Books on Demand GmbH, Norderstedt Germany
ISBN: 9783668357686

This book at GRIN:

http://www.grin.com/en/e-book/345715/how-can-self-learners-learn-programming-in-the-most-efficient-way-a-pragmatic

Sebastien Phlix

How can self-learners learn programming in the most efficient way? A pragmatic approach

GRIN Publishing

GRIN - Your knowledge has value

Since its foundation in 1998, GRIN has specialized in publishing academic texts by students, college teachers and other academics as e-book and printed book. The website www.grin.com is an ideal platform for presenting term papers, final papers, scientific essays, dissertations and specialist books.

Visit us on the internet:

http://www.grin.com/

http://www.facebook.com/grincom

http://www.twitter.com/grin_com

How can self-learners learn programming in the most efficient way? A pragmatic approach

by

Sébastien Phlix

HEC Entrepreneurs
B.Sc. Business Studies, University of Mannheim, 2013

Submitted in partial fulfillment of the requirements for the degree of

Master of Science in Management / Grande Ecole Diploma
at
HEC Paris

August 2016

How can self-learners learn programming in the most efficient way? A pragmatic approach

by
Sebastien Phlix – S50544
HEC Entrepreneurs – Promotion 2016

Submitted to HEC Paris / HEC Entrepreneurs
on August 31st, 2016

ABSTRACT

This paper provides a structured approach for self-learning programming for free on the internet. Its recommendations are based on a review of the existing academic literature which is complemented by the analysis of numerous contributions by software developers, self-learners, and teachers of programming. Additionally, it incorporates effective learning techniques derived from psychological research. Its intended readers are primarily entrepreneurs and 'startup people' who are driven to build new businesses with code, although the proposed approach is also transferable to other domains and audiences.

The single most important factor for succeeding in learning programming has been found to be of *human* nature: learner motivation and persistence. While most beginners and the majority of academic contributions focus mostly on *technical* aspects such as which language to learn first, or which learning resources to use, this paper analyzes the learning process itself. Learning programming is thus divided into three main steps: First, I highlight the importance of setting a strong learning goal for motivation, and provide a big-picture overview of what 'learning programming' encompasses to structure the approach. Second, I provide learners with recommendations as to which language to learn first – there is no one 'best' choice – as well as how and where to find effective learning resources. Lastly, the paper concludes with tips for optimizing the learning process by introducing effective learning techniques, highlighting the importance of programming practice, and collecting additional advice from programmers and self-learners.

Keywords: computing education, entrepreneurship, learning programming, learn to code, learning techniques, self-learning.

TABLE OF CONTENTS

1. INTRODUCTION

"Talk is cheap. Show me the code."

— Linus Torvalds

"We are in the middle of a dramatic and broad technological and economic shift in which software companies are poised to take over large swathes of the economy", writes Marc Andreessen in his influential 2011 essay titled "Why software is eating the world". Andreessen, a venture capitalist at AndreessenHorowitz (which invested in Facebook, Skype, and Twitter among others), goes on with saying that "more and more major businesses and industries are being run on software and delivered as online services". He cites many examples of software companies that took over whole industries: the world's largest bookseller is Amazon, the largest video service by number of subscribers is Netflix, the largest marketing platforms are Google and Facebook, etc. Today, we can see he was right, as his list could be complemented by many more recent examples like Uber, Airbnb or Tesla – and the list keeps growing. Most people will probably agree with Andreesen when he says that even more industries will be disrupted by software over the next ten years.

As a result, the opportunities for entrepreneurs are enormous, and they are everywhere. Uber started out in 2008, when its two co-founders were attending the LeWeb conference in Paris and hailing a cab proved to be a frustrating experience. They set out to solve this problem with technology and built a smartphone app to make transportation easier. Fast-forward 8 years later, and Uber's valuation is of a staggering $ 66 billion (Spiegel, 2016). With over two billion people now using the internet, up from perhaps 50 million a decade ago (Andreessen, 2011), entrepreneurs all over the world now have a chance to start a success story à la Uber of their own.

There is a major caveat, though: many people "lack the education and skills required to participate in the great new companies coming out of the software revolution" (Andreessen, 2011). The overwhelming majority of people did not study computer science and does not know how to program software that will "eat the world". They are so-called digital illiterates, and this is a major problem for entrepreneurs: How are they going to build out their revolutionary app idea if they do not have the skills to get started? How can they ask others to create their software idea when they have no idea how it works? How will they succeed when they do not know the time and effort involved in realizing their idea?

The answer is straightforward – entrepreneurs need to learn about programming. Broadly speaking, they have three options: getting a university degree, enrolling in a coding bootcamp, or studying on their own. While the first two options are great for people who can afford to spend at least a few weeks of in-person time and pay several thousand dollars upwards, that's certainly not the case for entrepreneurs – they have neither time nor money. Self-learning, on the other hand, allows learners to study at their own pace, from anywhere, and for free. It is flexible as the learning can be customized as needed. And while it remains an uncommon way of building skills in areas like business or law where most learning is formalized through certifications and degrees, it is a common way of learning programming: A recent poll on stack overflow* showed that 48% of software developers never received a degree in CS, and 33% of them never took a CS university course. Some of the most successful startups like Instagram and Tumblr were founded by self-taught programmers (Williams, 2015).

This has been made possible by a myriad of resources on the internet that offer programming education. Today, there are more than a thousand free programming books available to download. There are hundreds of free high-quality university courses on software engineering and computer science on the online MOOC platforms. There are dozens of programming tutorial companies that offer courses teaching hands-on programming knowledge – the internet provides "lifetimes-worth of programming knowledge and experience, available for free" (Larson, 2016a).

This paper intends to provide an actionable guide to make sense out of this enormous mass of resources for people who want to learn programming and build software to "eat the world". It is written primarily for entrepreneurs and "startup people" – they could be students who are thinking about becoming entrepreneurs, or employees at tech startups who want to gain a deeper understanding of the work technical teams do. In general, the approach taken is universal and can help anyone trying to learn programming. The research question to be answered is:

▶ How can self-learners learn programming in the most efficient way? ◀

This paper follows a practical, hands-on approach. While academic contributions are the foundation of this paper, additionally a large amount of real-life accounts and advice from the internet has been collected, analyzed, and put into perspective to ensure this paper's usefulness to self-learners of programming.

Accordingly, the paper follows the following structure: chapter 2 reviews the existing academic literature on learning programming. It covers the main challenges of self-directed learning (2.1), factors that make learning programming difficult (2.2), the lack of consensus on approaches to teaching programming (2.3), predictors of success in learning programming (2.4), choosing a first programming language (2.5), and the distinction between novice and expert programmers (2.6).

After the literature review, section 3.1 establishes the importance of setting a strong learning goal first instead of diving into tutorials right away (3.1.1). Subsequently, in 3.1.2, "programming" is broken down into manageable chunks of knowledge which are organized in four groups: the basics of web development, front-end development, back-end development, and problem solving. By doing so, the learning material is organized and readers are provided with an overview of what they will actually learn.

Section 3.2 structures the learning journey, beginning with the question of which programming language to learn first (3.2.1). It concludes that there is no one "best" choice and recommends learners to choose one of the three most common languages in web development today: JavaScript, Python, or Ruby. 3.2.2 then highlights the importance of establishing a curriculum to guide the learning and make sense of the vast quantity of available resources. It also provides a catalog of learning resources to choose from.

In section 3.3, learners are encouraged to optimize their learning routine. First, in 3.3.1 actionable learning techniques from psychological research are introduced. 3.3.2 then highlights the importance of programming practice. 3.3.3 ends the chapter with actionable advice from programmers, instructors, and self-learners to help learners avoid mistakes others have done before them.

Lastly, the paper concludes with an evaluation and critical discussion of findings (4.), and a final conclusion including suggestions for future research (5.).

2. LITERATURE REVIEW

In the past few years, the "Learn to Code" movement has advanced the idea that programming is the "new literacy" (Farag, 2016). It is supported by many industry leaders, celebrities, and politicians like New York City's mayor Michael Bloomberg who famously tweeted: "My New Year's resolution is to learn to code with Codecademy in 2012!" (BBC, 2012). Even though it has been successful in motivating millions of people to (try to) learn how to code, the phenomenon is still quite recent. For this reason, "little research is available that explains how adults undertaking online self-paced or instructional-based introductory courses experience learning code and outcomes" (Vivian, Falkner, & Szabo, 2014).

Instead, most of the academic research on learning programming has traditionally focused on university students, especially on first-year introductory computer science classes. This environment is clearly quite different from learning programming independently on the internet, which is why many findings of this research have to be analyzed carefully before drawing conclusions for self-learners. As a result, this chapter starts with a section on the specificities of self-learning (2.1). After that, it lays out the academic research which has focused on university students, with an emphasis on findings that are of direct relevance for self-learning programming. The findings are organized as follows: main factors that make learning programming difficult (2.2), a lack of consensus on approaches to teaching programming (2.3), predictors of student success in learning programming (2.4), choosing a first programming language for students (2.5), and lastly the distinction between novice and expert programmers (2.6).

2.1 Main challenges of self-directed learning

Before diving into the specificities of self-learning, it is helpful to establish a definition of what *learning* actually means. One of the most significant theories of how adult learners acquire skills is the five-step model developed by (Dreyfus & Dreyfus, 1986): after starting out as novice, the learner progresses through the stages of advanced beginner, competence, proficiency, until eventually becoming an expert. The process of learning skills is gradual, and skills are gained through instruction, practice, and apprenticeship. (Rogerson & Elsje, 2010) provide a good summary of how these stages are defined:

"During the novice stage, the student learns by the application of rules and following instructions. During the stage of advanced beginner, the learner starts to deal with practical situations and to recognize where to apply the previously learnt skills in an appropriate context. At this stage, the learner begins to draw from experience, but is still following instructions and learning by example. At the competence stage of learning, the learner is aware of the different ways of applying the rules and procedures to the situation at hand and must now make choices. The learners realize that not only is the outcome dependent on their own actions but they must also accept responsibility for those actions. It is this emotional involvement and experience that elevates the competent performer to the proficiency stage. To accomplish the desired outcome, the proficient learners must still decide what to do and may revert to following learned rules and procedures. To reach the fifth [expert] stage, the proficient performer must not only sense what needs to be done but also unconsciously know how to attain the desired result. The expert stage requires many years of practice and experience."

This theoretical underpinning of the learning process in general is useful to keep in mind when studying the process of self-learning programming.

Self-learning[1] is defined as "the act of learning about a subject or subjects in which one has had little to no formal education" (Wikipedia, 2016a). (Bolhuis, 1996) and (Garrison, 1997) add that "[self-learning] views learners as responsible owners and managers of their own learning process. [Self-learning] integrates self-management (management of the context, including the social setting, resources, and actions) with self-monitoring (the process whereby the learners monitor, evaluate and regulate their cognitive learning strategies)". Self-management means that learners are free to choose their learning goals, and the curriculum to get there. This freedom leaves a great amount of flexibility, but at the same time is a pitfall in many ways, which is discussed throughout this paper. (Garrison, 1997) notes the essential role of motivation and volition (i.e. willpower) for self-learners: "Motivation drives the decision to participate, and volition sustains the will to see a task through to the end so that goals are achieved".

Self-directed learning has the advantage of being available anywhere, anytime, and for free when compared to "traditional" classroom learning. Nonetheless, its approach also has drawbacks. First, self-learning online lacks the structure of classroom learning. For example, online classes often do not provide strict schedules (Elvers, Polzella, & Graetz, 2003). As a consequence, students need to be particularly self-disciplined and motivate themselves (Zhang & Perris, 2004). Because students are used to the structure and regularity of a classroom environment, it is hard for them to be fully responsible of their own learning. Second, self-learning does not offer a social community like classroom settings do. This can make students feel isolated

---

[1] Self-learning is also referred to as autodidactism, self-directed learning, self-education, or self-teaching.

from the class community (Zhang & Perris, 2004). It also makes it more difficult to identify knowledge gaps and misconceptions because learners communicate less with each other (Krause, Stark, & Mandl, 2009). Third, students cannot get immediate feedback from a teacher when they have a question (Zhang & Perris, 2004), which can be frustrating and decrease motivation. Lastly, many university students "often focus on topics associated with assessment and nothing else" (Gibbs & Simpson, 2004). Grades and diplomas provide an external motivation that self-learners do not have access to.

2.2 What makes learning programming difficult

This is the first of several sections covering the academic research that was conducted at universities, with a majority of studies focusing on introductory computer science courses. One of the few thoroughly established and undisputed findings seems to be that programming is considered to be a difficult task to the majority of students (Boyle, Carter, & Clark, 2002), (Jenkins, 2002), (Robins, Rountree, & Rountree, 2003), (Bergin & Reilly, 2005a), (Bergin & Reilly, 2005b), (Fincher, et al., 2006), (Gomes & Mendes, 2007a), and (Gomes & Mendes, 2007b).

These difficulties in students' learning have prevailed "despite great efforts during many decades to improve programming education" (Eckerdal, 2009). And, in the words of (Jenkins, 2002), "if students struggle to learn something, it follows that this thing is for some reason difficult to learn". (Anewalt, 2008) and (Porter & Calder, 2004) found that this difficulty has been a prime reason for students to drop out of their CS classes. There are many possible explanations as to why programming has proven to be so difficult for students. (Baldwin & Kuljis, 2001) attribute it to the fact that "learning programming demands complex cognitive skills such as planning, reasoning and problem-solving." Other studies provide more tangible factors of what makes learning how to program a difficult task. (Dann, Cooper, & Pausch, 2011) found four factors: (i) fragile mechanics of program creation, particularly syntax; (ii) the inability to see the result of computation as the program runs; (iii) the lack of motivation for programming; and (iv) the difficulty of understanding compound logic and learning design techniques. (Kelleher & Pausch, 2005) give another explanation: "In addition to the challenges of learning to form structured solutions to problems and understanding how programs are executed, beginning programmers also have to learn a rigid syntax and rigid commands that may have seemingly arbitrary or perhaps confusing names. Tackling all of these challenges simultaneously can be overwhelming and often discouraging for beginning programmers". A study by (Rogerson & Elsje, 2010) took the interesting approach of researching the challenges and difficulties of learning how to program as narrated by the students themselves. They found that most participants experience a literal "fear" of programming, which is in part attributed to the nature of programming. "Although these participants were motivated to succeed, the ensuing struggle resulted in

6

classic symptoms of procrastination and avoidance, which only added to the problem". Even though this particular study represents only a small sample size and does not allow for statistical generalization of findings, it shows what beginning self-learners should avoid: to become overwhelmed and intimidated by the sheer volume of concepts to study, and instead take a gradual approach that provides gratification along the way and thus helps to sustain self-efficacy and motivation. Another study by (Lahtinen, Ala-Mutka, & Järvinen, 2005) found that "the biggest problem of novice programmers does not seem to be the understanding of basic concepts but rather learning to apply them". In their study, "both students and teachers agreed that the practical learning situations were the most useful. Even if the theory is very important in learning programming, students also need practical experience to understand the concepts. The more practical and concrete the learning situations and materials are, the more learning takes place". This view has been widely shared by self-learners and practitioners, as we will see in chapter 3.3.2.

2.3 Lack of consensus on approaches to teaching programming

As learning programming has been found so difficult by many students, teaching a first programming course has been the subject of numerous studies, e.g. (Carter & Jenkins, 2002), (Kelleher & Pausch, 2005), (Pears, et al., 2007), (Ali & Mensch, 2008), (Hu, Winikoff, & Cranefield, 2012), (Verdú, et al., 2012), and (Combéfis, Beresnevicius, & Dagiene, 2016). There are many different approaches that propose new methodologies or frameworks for teaching programming, aiming to simplify the learning at beginner or entry-level for students who learn programming. (de Aquino Leal & Ferreira, 2016) remark that there is "no consensus on what is the best way for learning programming" in the academic world. This view is generally confirmed, e.g. by (Michaelson, 2015) who states that "70 years after the first computers were built, there is no well-established pedagogy for teaching programming", or (Pears, et al., 2007) who "conclude that despite the large volume of literature in this area, there is little systematic evidence to support any particular approach".

The lack of consensus today could have many reasons. As (Michaelson, 2015) notes, many studies were driven by "fashion, an enthusiastic or a wish to follow best industrial practice, which […] is poorly suited to novice programmers". An example of a study that was driven by fashion and, on top of that, was methodologically fragile, was (Amer & Ibrahim, 2014). They studied the effects of using an iPad in the classroom when teaching introductory programming, and measured the effectiveness of their approach simply by administering a student satisfaction survey (which turned out to yield moderately positive results). Another factor could be that there exists such a large number of teaching methods "it is difficult to keep up with them all" (Zendler, 2015) – (Gugel, 2011) cites 2,000 methods including their variations.

7

This paper thus focuses on a few selected studies with approaches that are interesting for self-learners, as they advocate the same principles many online-learning resources follow: (Herbert, 2007) proposes three factors to make learning how to program easier: minimize the syntax, provide visual feedback, and improve implementation and results. He clarifies that students should be 'gently' exposed to the new material, with more and more details being added over time. This point is important for self-learners since an effective way of gaining understanding of new concepts in programming is through metaphors and analogies which link the new material to familiar knowledge. Under sufficiently slow and gradual change, it works reasonably well; in the case of a sharp discontinuity, however, the method breaks down. (Dijkstra, 1989). (Baldwin & Kuljis, 2001) further suggest "designing the interface so that users can interact actively with it; using metaphors and analogies to explain concepts; and using spatial relationships so that users can develop capabilities for mental simulations". (Porter & Calder, 2004) note that students should be able to interact with the output of their programs, as this provides immediate feedback. If the output is made interesting, it can also help to keep students motivated. Another interesting approach by (McCartney, Eckerdal, Mostrom, Sanders, & Zander, 2007) asked students themselves what they would, in hindsight, recommend to succeed. The main points were to focus on practice, persistence, social networks, and step by step instructions. In general, most of the approaches introduced above have focused "on making the interaction attractive rather than identifying and diagnosing student motivation" (Thinakaran & Ali, 2016), which could explain why there is no consensus on a "best method" – the choice of method might be of secondary importance when compared to student motivation. The lack of research on student motivation in online environments, which is an essential question for self-learners, has been pointed out by (Thinakaran & Ali, 2016). Their paper was published two months before the time of writing of this paper, which indicates that this stream of research is still in its infancy. As of today, there remain a large variety of teaching approaches and a lack of consensus among academics.

As a side note that provides an entertaining insight in the sometimes 'special' world of programming, (Robins, Rountree, & Rountree, 2003) cite an "influential and completely different perspective on the art of teaching programming": (Dijkstra, 1989), in the evocatively titled ''On the cruelty of really teaching computer science'', argues that anthropomorphic metaphors, graphical programming environments and the like are misleading and represent an unacceptable "dumbing down" of the process. He proposes a different kind of curriculum based on mathematical foundations such as predicate calculus and Boolean algebra, and establishing formal proofs of program correctness.

2.4 Predictors of success in learning programming

There is a large number of studies trying to determine predictors of success among students, e.g. (Byrne & Lyons, 2001), (McCracken, et al., 2001), (Wilson & Shrock, 2001), (Bergin & Reilly, 2005a), (Fincher, et al., 2006), (Gomes & Mendes, 2007a), (Gomes & Mendes, 2007b), and (Kinnunen, McCartney, Murphy, & Thomas, 2007). An indicative list of twelve factors has been established in (Wilson & Shrock, 2001), including: previous programming experience, previous non-programming experience, work style preference, math background, gender, the student's own attribution for success or failure, and the student's level of comfort. Their conclusion was that, of all the variables, comfort level was the most reliable predicator of success. Low levels of comfort often result in feelings of anxiety, which is counterproductive to learning and may result in a dislike of programming as a discipline (Fincher, et al., 2006).

Other studies focused on inherent factors such as gender, age, culture, and language. Interestingly, their findings were so varied that no reliable predictors emerged (Byrne & Lyons, 2001), (Jenkins, 2002), and (Kinnunen, McCartney, Murphy, & Thomas, 2007). The only exception is intelligence: it seems to be generally established that measures of general intelligence are related to success at learning to program (Mayer, Dyck, & Vilberg, 1986). I view this finding as encouraging: students have it in their hands to work on improving the skills that will allow them to become good programmers, without being disadvantaged by factors they cannot control. One example is gender: While the majority of programmers and programming students are male (Stack Overflow, 2016), (unsurprisingly) "female students achieved equally high scores as their male counterparts (Byrne & Lyons, 2001), which was confirmed in (Carter & Jenkins, 2002).

As noted in (Gomes & Mendes, 2007a, 2007b), poor problem solving ability frequently is the number one cause of failure amongst programming students, which suggests that being good at problem solving could be a major predictor of success when learning programming. Several authors have taken a comparable approach and focused on which specific topics, apart from problem solving, need to be learned by students to succeed in introductory programming courses. (Dann, Cooper, & Pausch, 2011) name three of them: algorithm thinking, abstraction, and appreciation of elegance. (Winslow, 1996) adds that "studies have shown that there is very little correspondence between the ability to write a program and the ability to read one. Both need to be taught along with some basic test and debugging strategies". (Soloway & Spohrer, 1989) note that "students are not given sufficient instruction in how to 'put the pieces together.' Focusing explicitly on specific strategies for carrying out the coordination and integration of the goals and plans that underlie program code may help to reverse this trend." (Berglund & Eckerdal, 2015) make a similar point when they say that students need to "learn both the theoretical aspects of programming (for example the meaning of an if-clause, the idea methods) more or less at the same time as they learn the practical aspects (the handicraft, such as where to put semicolon, how to act on error messages)". In a more holistic approach that is generally accepted, (McGill & Volet, 1997) summarize the three types of skills that learners need to acquire: The first is syntactic knowledge, i.e. knowledge about a programming language and the rules for its use. Second, conceptual knowledge concerns constructs and principles of computer programming. As (Baldwin & Kuljis, 2001) point out, with "both syntactic and conceptual knowledge, learners are able to design solutions to simple, or closely-related, problems that they have met in the classroom." Third, strategic knowledge concerns general problem-solving skills which are program-specific. (Baldwin & Kuljis, 2001) comment that "with syntactic, conceptual and strategic knowledge learners are able to solve novel programming problems. It is strategic knowledge that is needed for the recognition and decomposition of a problem, as well as for testing and debugging errors, as well as designing the phases of programming." (Kinnunen, McCartney, Murphy, & Thomas, 2007) added that students' study methods were also a determining factor of success, which is why this paper devotes its chapter 3.3 to identify effective study methods for learning programming.

Psychological attitudes, too, have been found to be predictors of success: motivation and attitude to learning, as well as believing in oneself and one's abilities, which is known as self-efficacy (Gomes & Mendes, 2007b), (Jenkins, 2002), (McCartney, Eckerdal, Mostrom, Sanders, & Zander, 2007), and (Robins, Rountree, & Rountree, 2003). "Emotions and perceptions play a role in learning to program, as it was found that students who demonstrated optimistic attributions to learning were found to perform better than those with less optimistic views and, further, students who reasoned that positive events were attributed to the self (internal factors) and unchangeable (e.g. ability) had better grades than students with pessimistic attributions" (Vivian, Falkner, & Szabo, 2014). Additionally, "whilst effort, attitude and other internal factors are recognized by participants, persistence – although not unique to programming – is a quality that is recommended if students are to succeed at programming" (Vivian, Falkner, & Szabo, 2014).

Lastly, a strand of literature found that having prior programming experience is a clear predictor of success (Hagan & Markham, 2000), (Byrne & Lyons, 2001), (Bergin & Reilly, 2005a), and (Capovilla, Berges, Mühling, & Hubwieser, 2015). While this finding is interesting, it does not help the beginning learners which are the focus of this paper – it can rather be seen as an encouragement to get started and program as much as possible.

2.5 Choice of the first programming language

A large body of literature focuses on which language to choose for beginning learners. They study many different languages and offer a wide range of possible conclusions. In the academic world, Python is relatively common as it offers many libraries that can be used in scientific contexts (e.g. data science / statistics). In study that compared C++ and Python, (Ateeq, Habib, Umer, & Rehman, 2014) favor Python because of the "simpler pseudocodish syntax, easy to learn environment and higher abstraction". (Yadin, 2011) adds that Python's easy syntax allowed the students to focus on improving their problem-solving skills and algorithmic thinking. Python is now taught at 8 of the top 10 computer science in the US, and seems to have a promising future as a first programming language. There are several other authors like (Leping, et al., 2009) in favor of Python as a first programming language.

In general, however, there is no consensus on which first programming language to choose – a large number of studies favors an equally large number of languages. (Holvikivi, 2010) advocates JavaScript because "its easy syntax and applicability on [the] Web" help to motivate the students. Others, like (Winslow, 1996) and some contributors in (Soloway & Spohrer, 1989), suggest the use of simple, specially designed teaching languages for beginners. Examples include Alice, Kara, Scratch, Pascal, or BASIC. (McIver, 2000) introduced a new language called GRAIL, which she found to be superior than LOGO. Some authors favor the use of an industrial strength programming language, e.g. Java, C/C++, FORTRAN or COBOL (Michaelson, 2015) – the list could go on. While these findings seem to be contradictory and non-conclusive, it helps to take a step back to consolidate the research:

> "The use of 'safer' or more managed languages and environments can help scaffold students' learning. But, such languages may provide a level of abstraction that obscures an understanding of actual machine execution and makes is difficult to evaluate performance trade-offs. The decision as to whether to use a 'lower-level' language to promote a particular mental model of program execution that is closer to the actual execution by the machine is often a matter of local audience needs. The use of a language or environment designed for introductory pedagogy can facilitate student learning, but may be of limited use beyond CS1. Conversely, a language or environment commonly used professionally may expose students to too much complexity too soon." (Association for Computing Machinery (ACM), 2013).

As a summary, programming languages are not good or bad per se; they are good or bad for a specific purpose that will depend on the individual self-learner's goals.

2.6 What distinguishes novice and expert programmers

A large body of work has focused on determining the differences between beginners in programming, termed 'novices', and experts. In general, the literature agrees that it takes about 10 years to turn a beginner into an expert programmer (Winslow, 1996). (Rist, 1995) summarizes the advantages of expert programmers as follows: "Expertise in programming should reduce variability in three ways: by defining

11

the best way to approach the design task, by supplying a standard set of schemas to answer a question, and by constraining the choices about execution structure to the 'best' solutions". (Robins, Rountree, & Rountree, 2003) add that experts are "good at recognizing, using and adapting patterns or schemas (and thus obviating the need for much explicit work or computation). They are faster, more accurate, and able to draw on a wide range of examples, sources of knowledge, and effective strategies".

As for novices, (Winslow, 1996) have concluded they are limited to surface and superficially organized knowledge, lack detailed mental models, fail to apply relevant knowledge, and approach programming "line by line" rather than using meaningful program "chunks" or structures: "[An important point] is the large number of studies concluding that novice programmers know the syntax and semantics of individual statements, but they do not know how to combine these features into valid programs. Even when they know how to solve the problems by hand, they have trouble translating the hand solution into an equivalent computer program". (Soloway & Spohrer, 1989) add novices' lack of understanding of various specific programming language constructs (such as variables, loops, arrays and recursion), note shortcomings in their planning and testing of code, show how prior knowledge can be a source of errors, and more. These findings are useful in providing an indication of which higher-level skills are important for self-learners to become better at programming.

A recent contribution has acknowledged the existence of a seemingly obvious, but previously widely ignored third group: so-called "conversational programmers". They do not intend to become professional programmers, but want to gain a basic literacy in programming so they can "speak in the 'programmer's language" and improve their job prospects in the software industry (Chilana, et al., 2015).

3. SELF-LEARNING PROGRAMMING

After having reviewed the academic literature, this chapter provides actionable guidelines for self-learners to make their learning more efficient. It is structured in three parts that follow the actual learning process: first, learners set a learning goal for themselves and get a first overview of the material they want to learn (3.1). Then, they structure their learning journey by choosing a first programming language and deciding on which learning resources to use (3.2). Lastly, they are encouraged to optimize their learning by incorporating findings from psychological learning research in their study routine, by focusing on 'learning by doing', and by taking advantage of advice from expert programmers and other self-learners (3.3).

3.1 Setting a learning goal and getting a first overview

This section takes the broad aspiration of "I want to learn programming", and breaks it down into an actionable goal and manageable chunks of material to study. When learners start learning programming, many of them simply pick a tutorial or MOOC and jump right into it. This approach has a major drawback: it is impossible to track your progress if you just set out to "learn programming" – how will you measure your progress on that? Tutorials and MOOCs have metrics like "you completed 87% of the Python track", but does that actually mean something to you personally? You need to set a clear goal for yourself first, so that you can assess if you are progressing or not (3.1.1). After having set a goal, it is helpful to gain an overview of what languages and technologies the broad term "programming" actually encompasses (3.1.2).

3.1.1 The importance of learning goals for motivation

Keeping up your motivation in an online learning context is especially difficult due to the easy-to-procrastinate nature of online learning (Elvers, Polzella, & Graetz, 2003) – Facebook is only one click away, there is no fixed schedule, and no teacher to hold you accountable. In MOOCs, for example, the average completion rate is below 13% (Onah, Sinclair, & Boyatt, 2014). To overcome this lack of motivation, the most often recommended strategy is to set a strong learning goal for yourself. "Don't learn programming just for the sake of it, or because you've heard it's cool and it pays well. Do it because you want to solve your own problems" (Soare, 2015). Without a strong goal in mind, you are much more likely to give up along the way by making excuses like "you don't like programming anymore, [...] programming is not for you, or [...] you weren't born to be a programmer. If you have a project in mind, or a higher problem that you want to solve, you can say to yourself: 'This might not be an enjoyable experience right now, but I really want to solve this bigger problem, so I'm going to push myself and overcome this obstacle'" (Soare, 2015). This intuition has been confirmed by academic research: goals are very closely linked to motivation, so both long and short term goals help keep learners moving through their different types of study (Boyes, 2003).

An example of an effective long-term goal could be to reach the ability to build and deploy a simple web application to test a business idea and find first customers. This is an actionable goal that you can actually achieve. You can break it down into smaller goals, and measure progress – as opposed to "I want to learn programming" (too vague), or "I want to learn Python" (better, but still too vague). You should also avoid overly ambitious goals, such as "I want to build a better social networking site because I don't like Facebook" (too ambitious). Having a well-chosen and strong long-term goal in mind helps you stay motivated and persist in your learning: by knowing what you want to achieve, you know what you have to concentrate on and improve. This has been confirmed in many accounts of self-taught programmers. (Pash, 2009) states that "rather than simply a good idea, what you really need is an idea you're passionate about". He wanted to make and share playlists online, but was unhappy with the existing solutions – so he established a goal for himself: create a better solution, although he did not know how to program. But he was "really excited about the idea, so spending time learning, researching, and working on it in [his] spare time was almost always a lot of fun—even when [he] was banging [his] head against the wall trying to figure out why something wasn't working." He ended up teaching himself to program and built a functional web application that satisfied his needs. (Carver, 2013) recommends that "before you learn to code, think about what you want to code. Knowing how to code is mostly about building things, and the path is a lot clearer when you have a sense of the end goal. If your goal is 'learn to code,' without a clear idea of the kinds of programs you will write and how they will make your life better, you will probably find it a frustrating exercise." Without a strong goal in mind, "you will end up chasing your tail learning all kinds of interesting but ultimately unproductive things" (Trautman, 2015b). Lastly, (Trautman, 2015a) adds that a "deep well of genuine passion for what you're studying [...] can be critical to help you to pick yourself up after the inevitable stumbles. It keeps you fully engaged with the material instead of feeling like learning is an obligation."

Once you have established a strong long-term learning goal, it can then be broken down into smaller, more short-term goals. This process is often referred to as Swiss cheese method (Boyes, 2003). Gradually moving towards the overarching goal brings "a great sense of completion and satisfaction" (Oakley, 2014), i.e. helps to stay motivated. It also helps with planning time by providing more manageable chunks. As a summary, goals are essential for motivation as they help you break larger, intimidating aspirations into smaller, more achievable stepping stones.

3.1.2 What "learning how to program" encompasses

After having defined a learning goal, the next question arises: what skills and languages are needed to reach that goal? This paper focuses on web development, as this encompasses the programming skills that most entrepreneurs will likely need to advance their business, whether it be selling physical products in a web shop, building a business-to-business SaaS application, or setting up a landing page to collect email addresses. These are also the topics that most engineering teams work on at existing tech companies, and will therefore be of use to employees wishing to improve their technical understanding. Web development is defined as "the process and technology of creating websites" by (Cambridge University Press, 2011). (Wikipedia, 2016) specifies that web development "can range from developing the simplest static single page of plain text to the most complex web-based internet applications, electronic businesses, and social network services". This definition is already a lot clearer than simply saying you want to learn "coding" or "programming". Such a broader definition would encompass a wider range of skills, such as machine learning, data science, artificial intelligence, or game design. While all of these fields are certainly rewarding, it is beyond the scope of this paper to cover them all. Nonetheless, the general approach towards learning taken here should be useful for people wanting to learn any of these topics. Now that we established our focus on web development, there is still a vast amount of programming languages, frameworks, and tools to choose from. The next sections will provide you with an overview of the most common ones that are used to build websites. It starts with basic knowledge about web development (3.1.2.1), goes on to front-end development (3.1.2.2), covers the back-end (3.1.2.3), and ends with problem solving (3.1.2.4). This approach roughly follows (Stern, 2016) and was complemented by (White, 2016) and (The Odin Project, 2016). Its goal is to delimitate what we are talking about when talking about "learning programming" by naming the most relevant languages, technologies, and skills.

All of these skills listed together might seem overwhelming at first. Nonetheless, it is useful to get a glimpse of the whole web stack – how else would you choose which ones to study to reach your goal? Only after having reached a basic understanding of what is out there can you choose which skills and languages you want to focus on. Additionally, the following list can be used to structure all the material that is needed to reach your individual learning goal – "the only way to walk a journey of a thousand miles is to take one step at a time" (Oakley, 2014).

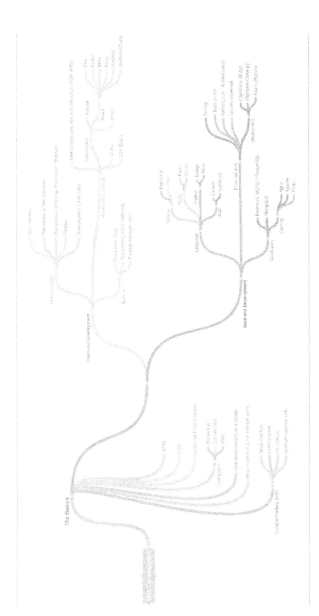

Figure 1: What programming encompasses

3.1.2.1 The basics

Knowing the basics of web development primarily means being familiar with HTML, CSS, and elementary JavaScript. In the following paragraphs, I also included elementary knowledge of web development as a career, basic knowledge of the internet and how computers work, and necessary complementary skills like the command line and version control.

Learning about the basics of web development serves different purposes. First, it will teach learners the most basic languages and concepts of web development. There really is no way around them, as everything else builds on knowing these essentials. Second, it helps to familiarize learners with what is called the "full stack", i.e. all the different areas of web development and what they mean. Lastly, as (Trautman, 2015a) points out, the first time spent learning web development should be used to "find your coding match so you can passionately dive into that area". It is important to get a sense of which technologies you enjoy most before picking a language or technology, as you will spend countless hours working with them in the future.

HTML, CSS, AND ELEMENTARY JAVASCRIPT

No matter if you are on an iPhone, Google Chrome, or an old version of Internet Explorer, your browser will be putting together an HTML page with CSS styling, and adding functionalities through JavaScript. These three languages – HTML, CSS, and JavaScript – are the basic building blocks of web development, and essential to know for anyone looking to learn web development. jQuery is a widely used JavaScript library that is targeted at web development, and can thus be useful to check out as well. As program code is written in text editors, you will need to choose a text editor to work with; the three most common ones today are Atom.io, Sublime Text, and Brackets.io.

WEB DEVELOPMENT AS A CAREER

Leaners should know what the actual practice of web development is all about. (The Odin Project, 2016) gives a comprehensive overview of what this includes: First, it means knowing what a developer actually does in his job, as well as being able to distinguish between front-end and back-end. Second, you should get a grasp on web development jobs and careers to understand what developer roles are like in a variety of different organizations. It can also be useful to get to know communities of web developers, both online and offline. Third, it means knowing the "tools of the trade", i.e. the tools that web developers use to get their work done. Lastly, for people who are looking to work in web development themselves or looking to hire a web developer, it is worth knowing what employers are usually looking for in a web developer and what the typical hiring process looks like.

After having idea of what 'web development' encompasses, you should gain a basic understanding of how computers and the internet work. Computers are composed of four basic parts (input, output, CPU, and memory), which you should be roughly familiar with. You should also know what binary code means and how data size and speed are measured. When it comes to knowing how the internet works, you should be familiar with the client-server model and the HTTP protocol. In both of these domains, there are many more interesting topics to learn.

First, many authors recommend you should be able to use the terminal, also called command line. (Hoffman, 2010) summarizes why:

> "The command-line interface, sometimes referred to as the CLI, is a tool into which you can type text commands to perform specific tasks—in contrast to the mouse's pointing and clicking on menus and buttons. Since you can directly control the computer by typing, many tasks can be performed more quickly, and some tasks can be automated with special commands that loop through and perform the same action on many files—saving you, potentially, loads of time in the process. The application or user interface that accepts your typed responses and displays the data on the screen is called a shell, and there are many different varieties that you can choose from."

The command line looks scary to newcomers, because it does not use the point-and-click interface we are used to today. However, there are only 10-20 commands needed to get started with it, so it is not as hard to learn as it seems.

Second, you should learn basic version control with Git. Version control keeps track of the changes to your code, and allows you do things like undo coding errors and see what has changed in the code over time. It also allows you to work easily with other programmers on the same code. As a result, Git is considered an essential skill for any web developer to have. GitHub is the code hosting platform that goes with it – "if you are a developer today, you MUST have a GitHub account" (Sourour, 2016).

Third, you should become familiar with researching programming concepts on your own. You will perform Google searches all the time when programming. The most important website you need to know for this is called Stack Overflow[2]. Stack Overflow is a question and answer site for professional and enthusiast programmers which covers a wide range of topics in computer programming. "Every problem you have in

---

[2] The satirical online blog 'The Allium' published a post titled "Computer Programming To Be Officially Renamed 'Googling Stackoverflow'" which ended up being shared more than 100,000 times.

the first year you learn to program is a problem 100 other people have had before you. And all the answers are recorded online. The sooner you become effective at googling for programming help, the happier you'll be. Caveat: Don't ever take any code snippets you find online if you don't understand how they work" (Gentle, 2014).

Lastly, an essential thing to know about is browser inspector tools. If you use Chrome, the tool is called 'Developer Tools'. Inspector tools are used to "see the source code of web pages" or "track JavaScript as it executes, print debug statements to the console, and see things like network requests and resources." (White, 2016). If there is an error in the code, the inspector console will (in most cases) point to the particular line of code where the error is, making it easier to find and fix errors which is essential for beginners.

After having learned all the basics introduced above, you can choose to deepen your understanding of front-end development, or move on to back-end development.

3.1.2.2 Front-end development

The front-end of the web is the part that you can see and interact with. As (Long, 2012) puts it, "everything that you see when using the web is a combination of HTML, CSS, and JavaScript all being controlled by your computer's browser." Front-end development is thus the task of programming HTML, CSS and JavaScript so that when users open up a website, they see the information in a format that is easy to read and relevant. A common challenge of front-end developers is to ensure that a website comes up correctly in different devices, browsers, and operating systems ('responsive'). This can be quite complex as people today use a large variety of devices with screen sizes ranging from small smartphones to large iMacs (Wikipedia, 2016c).

If you want to build on the basics from the previous chapter and become a better front-end developer, there are three main topics you should learn about: proficient CSS, proficient JavaScript for the front-end, and so-called build tools to optimize the development workflow.

PROFICIENT CSS

CSS is easy to pick up in the beginning, but can become relatively complex when building websites, especially responsive ones. For this reason, there are CSS frameworks that allow creating responsive websites quickly and easily. The most common ones are Bootstrap and Foundation, and to a lesser extent Skeleton, Bourbon Neat, and Gumby. Some frameworks like Bootstrap also provide ready-to-use page elements like buttons or modals, which makes the creation of new websites faster. You should be familiar with at least one of those. Many practitioners also recommend learning how to build responsive designs

19

with pure CSS with techniques such as media queries, flexbox, and responsive images. This allows for more flexibility and deeper understanding (Stern, 2016).

Another recommended skill to learn is CSS pre-compilers. They allow putting more functionalities to CSS, such as defining global variables for colors. The two most common ones are SASS and, to a lesser extent and with decreasing popularity, LESS. They usually take a day or less to learn, and can be very useful. Nonetheless, not every project requires them as illustrated in (Thornton, 2014).

Lastly, you should get familiar with best practices such as semantic markup, i.e. "using appropriate HTML tags and meaningful CSS class names to convey structural meaning" (White, 2016); CSS naming conventions that help make code predictable, readable, and maintainable; and CSS resets to overcome small styling inconsistencies between browsers.

PROFICIENT JAVASCRIPT FOR THE FRONT-END

For websites that are more or less static, it is enough to use rudimentary JavaScript or jQuery to add basic functionality. However, in order to be able to do more advanced things and understand what is going on "under the hood", you should learn more about JavaScript. The first step is to gain a better understanding of the language and its syntax. This means grasping concepts like "variable instantiation, loops, and functions" and object-oriented programming (White, 2016). The next step is to apply this knowledge to the web by learning about the Document Object Model (DOM). Simply put, when a browser receives an HTML file from your server, it turns it into the DOM. JavaScript then interacts with the DOM and can change it. Another important concept is API calls with AJAX and JSON, i.e. getting data from third-party websites to power your web application.

Once this intermediate knowledge is gained, you can pick up a JavaScript framework. Frameworks help to structure and organize code. They provide developers with repeatable solutions to complex front-end problems and are commonly used to build web apps. According to (Stern, 2016), the first framework to learn today is React, which is a relatively new framework backed by Facebook. React works with Flux, Facebook's architecture for creating data layers in JavaScript applications. Another very popular framework has been Angular.js which is backed by Google. However, according to (Stern, 2016), it has been struggling with the introduction of its latest version which has gained mixed reviews in the web developer community. A large-scale survey (JavaScript Scene, 2015) confirms this: "Almost half (45%) [of respondents] currently use Angular, and more than half (66%) are interested in React. There are fewer people interested in Angular than using Angular, and that may spell a pending decline in Angular use. Angular currently dominates the front end component library landscape, but judging by these results, React seems poised to give Angular a run for its money in the coming months." Other, although far less popular, frameworks that learners could choose to learn are Ember.js or Vue.js.

FRONT-END BUILD TOOLS

Build tools are used to improve the development workflow, which is important for web development as it saves a lot of time. The development workflow can be broken down into six parts, as summarized in (Liew, 2015):

1. "Scaffold is where you setup your web project. This is where you'll create a git repo, prepare file structures, download libraries and dependencies and all other tasks just to make sure your project is ready to go.
2. Develop is where you spend the most of your time - writing code!
3. Test is where you test to see if your code works. You'll go back and develop more if things aren't working out, or if your new code breaks some other stuff on your website.
4. Integrate is where you merge your code with the rest of your team. This usually involves merging git branches. You skip integration if you work solo.
5. Optimize is where you prepare all your assets for use on the production server. Files are optimized such that they allow your visitors to view your site as quickly as possible.
6. Deploy is where you push your code and assets up into the server and allow changes to be viewed by the public."

Build tools optimize the workflow. The first kind of tools that are typically used by web developers are task runners. They enable code to be broken down into multiple files, make it easier to avoid conflicts, and avoid a lot of time-consuming repetitive tasks like concatenating or prefixing. They also improve page speed by decreasing the number of files requested per page load and compressing files. The two main task runners are Grunt and Gulp, although Gulp is the preferred choice for most developers today (Stern, 2016). Another important tool is Webpack, which is used for JavaScript dependency management. If JavaScript code is spread out over multiple files, the developer needs to manage the dependencies between them, which is mostly done with Webpack. A common alternative is Browserify. Lastly, learners should know about package managers. Packages are collections of code that developers have created to solve particular problems. npm allows JavaScript developers to re-use that code in their own applications, and has become a standard tool for front-end developers.

3.1.2.3 Back-end development

The back-end of a website usually consists of three parts: a server, an application, and a database. (Long, 2012) provides a good explanation of what this means:

"If you book a flight or buy concert tickets, you usually open a website and interact with the frontend. Once you've entered that information, the *application* stores it in a *database* that was created on a *server*. For sake of ease, just think about a database as a giant Excel spreadsheet on your computer, but your computer (server) is stored somewhere in Arizona. All of that information stays on the server so when you log back into the application to print your tickets, all of the information is still there in your account."

Back-end web developers are the people that build all of this technology to work together. Backend technologies usually consist of languages, and frameworks that enhance the languages to make development faster. The languages that are used most in web development are PHP, Ruby, Node.js (i.e. JavaScript), and Python. PHP developers mostly use the Laravel or Symfony2 frameworks. Ruby is generally used with Rails or Sinatra. Node.js is often used with Express.js or Hapi. Python is generally used with Django or Flask. In general, learners will choose one language and then stick with it until they become 'good' in it – the question which language to choose will be discussed in chapter 3.2.1. Other languages that are less used in web development are high-performance or compiled languages like Go / GoLang, Java, C, and C#, or functional languages like Elixir, Scala, Clojure, and Haskell.

No matter which language the learner has chosen, there are several skills to have in order to become proficient in that language. (Stern, 2016) suggests that you need to know how to test your code. Additionally, you should know how to build an API in the language of choice. You also should know how to handle security, authorization, and authentication which includes OAUTH2 and JSON WebToken. Lastly, you need to know how to deploy your application to the web, i.e. pushing the application to the internet and making it available to the public. There are many platforms to do that, and you should be familiar with at least one of them. Popular choices are Flightplan for Node.js, Fabric for Python, or Capistrano for Ruby.

To store the data from your app, you will tie it to a database. There a many different types of databases to choose from, but (Stern, 2016) suggests to start learning about so-called relational databases. This means learning MySQL first, and then PostgreSQL which provides more advanced features. A popular alternative to relational databases is MongoDB, which is often used with Node.js. Additionally, you could learn about caching, which helps storing data temporarily so that the database needs to be called less often. On the server level, these are Nginx or Apache, and on the database level you can pick up Redis.

3.1.2.4 Problem solving

Part of learning programming, as described in the previous paragraphs, is learning a language's syntax and the tools commonly used by developers. But a much bigger part of learning programming, "the part that takes longer and gives you more headaches, is learning to solve problems like a programmer" (Christensen, 2015). (Grover, 2013) writes about learners "who have ostensibly marched through an entire JavaScript course online but struggle […] with a fairly simple program. […] While not so drastic, it is somewhat akin to confusing architecture with construction". You need to understand not only the syntax and semantics of a language, but also how to systematically break down a problem and then compose an algorithmic solution – you need to study problem solving.

Problem solving consists of using generic or ad hoc methods, in an orderly manner, for finding solutions to problems (Wikipedia, 2016d). In her influential article, (Wing, 2006) introduced the idea of "computational thinking" to apply problem solving to computers, which in essence means "thinking like a computer scientist" when confronted with a problem. A more actionable definition has been proposed by (Kao, 2011), who outlines a "set of skills that software engineers use" to solve problems:

1. Decomposition: the ability to break down a problem into sub-problems.
2. Pattern recognition: the ability to notice similarities, differences, properties, or trends in data.
3. Pattern generalization: the ability to extract unnecessary details and generalize those that are necessary in order to define a concept or idea in general terms.
4. Algorithm design: the ability to build a repeatable, step-by-step process to solve a particular problem.

These clear steps are helpful in creating a general framework, but still offer only limited guidance for how to apply them in solving concrete problems. (Hilton, 2016) provides a more practical approach to solve programming problems:

1. Work the example by hand, i.e. work simplified versions of the problem.
2. Write down what you did, step-by-step.
3. Find patterns to devise an algorithm[3].
4. Check by hand if the algorithm works for all cases.
5. Translate to code.
6. Run test cases.
7. Debug failed test cases.

When confronted with a more complex problem, before using that methodology, some larger problems can be divided into simpler, analogous pieces, and solved by combining solutions to the simpler pieces. This technique is referred to as "divide and conquer" and commonly used by programmers (Sonmez, 2011). For example, let's say you want to build a rock-paper-scissors game. If you break this problem apart, it consists

---

[3] An algorithm is defined as "a self-contained step-by-step set of operations to be performed" (Wikipedia, 2016g).

of several sub-problems: how to get input from the user, how to make the computer pick a random option, how to tell who won, and how to repeat the entire thing. Keep breaking up your problems into smaller and smaller pieces, and research things that seem irreducible.

There are many more problem solving strategies and techniques worth exploring that can help with programming - good places to start for self-learners are described in 3.3.2. What you should keep in mind is that problem solving is an essential skill for programming, and you need to study it just as much as language syntax.

3.2 Structuring the learning journey

After having set a goal for learning and having seen what skills are needed to reach it comes the time to actually start learning. Being a self-learner means there is no mentor to ask "where should I start?" and no professor to provide homework assignments – you need to figure it out all by yourself. (Trautman, 2015a) describes what typically happens when a beginner asks for advice on learning to program:

"Try Python. At first you'll be just fooling around, but then in 15 minutes you'll be intrigued and after an hour you'll wonder where the time went!"

"I don't recommend python as a first programming language to learn... Java is the perfect starting spot."

"Learn Java or C++ then take Stanford's online class in iOS app development."

"Which programming language you learn and use doesn't matter."

"Learn code with a project in mind"

"Just type what you see in the book"

His list goes on with more examples, but these are enough to prove his point: "if you ask a dozen different people how to get started, you will probably receive 15 different answers. Ask the Internet and you'll find that it's rife with giant SEO-friendly listicles packed full of resources for learning how to code [...] and occasionally even a few tips about how to navigate through them. The dilemma comes when you're faced with all those reasonable-seeming approaches and need to choose between them or risk wasting your time. The problem, therefore, isn't a lack of resources or even a path, it's a set of criteria for figuring out which path makes the most sense for you to take". In short, after having defined a goal for learning, you need to choose which languages and technologies to learn (3.2.1), and to decide on which free resources to use (3.2.2) in order to learn in the most effective way.

3.2.1 Picking a first programming language

One of the most popular questions that self-learners ask on various forums on the internet is what language to learn first. Their question is often based on a common misconception: that there actually is a "best" programming language for learning – in reality, there is no one best language to start with. Some people will recommend Python (Barba, 2014), while others swear by JavaScript (Fullstack Academy, 2016), Ruby (Atwood, Why Ruby?, 2013), or C (Spolsky, 2005). An exception is mobile development, where the choice is easy: if your goal is to make iPhone apps, the only language to do so is Swift, and for Android apps it is Java. When it comes to web development, however, you need to choose between several popular languages. (Norvig, 2001) points out that the goal of your first programming language is two-fold: first, it should teach you the basic concepts of programming, like data types, control structures, etc. Second, it should allow you to accomplish your personal project in order for you to stay interested and motivated. Additionally, many programmers advise to pick a language with a relatively forgiving syntax, immediately visible results, and a light-weight or non-existing IDE[4] (MacDonald, 2013). Lastly, an important factor to be considered is the size of the community around a language. (Codementor, 2016a) writes that "the larger a programming language community is, the more support you'd be likely to get. […] Moreover, the larger a community, the more people will be building useful tools to make development in that particular language easier". With this in mind, in the next paragraphs, I shortly introduce the programming languages that are most popular for beginners – JavaScript, Python, Ruby, PHP, Java, C, C#, and the so-called 'beginner languages'[5].

JavaScript is *the* language for front-end development as it runs in every browser on the web. It can also be used as a server-side scripting language to power the back-end of a web application through the Node.js platform (thus the term 'full-stack JavaScript'). Facebook's popular React Native framework allows to build native mobile apps for both iOS and Android with pure JavaScript, which makes it a very versatile language – you need it for your front-end anyway, and you can power the back-end as well as the mobile app with it. According to (MacDonald, 2013), JavaScript has a comparatively "forgiving" syntax. Additionally, "because the code runs in the browser, it has more visual punch than running in a terminal window…even if the output is just text, seeing it in a browser, like a 'proper' web page, has a more satisfying effect." There are abundant resources and support available for learners as JavaScript has a large community. Because of its widespread use and popularity, JavaScript boasts many frameworks and libraries such as the previously mentioned React, jQuery, and Angular.js. These frameworks, most notably Angular

---

[4] An integrated development environment (IDE) is a software suite that consolidates the basic tools developers need to write and test software. Typically, an IDE contains a code editor, a compiler or interpreter and a debugger.
[5] HTML and CSS (which, technically speaking, are no real programming languages) are not mentioned here as they will be learned anyway. They are the first steps you take when learning about web development, no matter which scripting language you wish to pursue.

and React, allow developers to build so-called 'single-page' web applications that do not require a page refresh at every step and have thus set new standards in user experience (e.g. Gmail or Facebook). For this reason, the most regarded coding bootcamps have "come to the conclusion that full-stack JavaScript is the future of web development" (Fullstack Academy, 2016), and decided to focus purely on teaching full-stack JavaScript accordingly. While many programmers will wholeheartedly disagree with this view, most do agree on the fact that the importance of JavaScript will be increasing in the future. Another argument in the favor of learning full-stack JavaScript is that if students decide to pick up another language, they have to do a lot of switching between languages for different parts of the stack (e.g. JavaScript for the front-end, Ruby for the back-end, and SQL for the database). Full-stack JavaScript eliminates this problem and saves beginners valuable learning time spent grappling with syntax since every part only uses JavaScript. As a conclusion, JavaScript is a very popular choice as a first programming language.

Python is considered relatively easy to learn because it looks closer to the English language when compared with many other programming languages. It is a versatile language: you can build websites, analyze data, or maintain servers (Barba, 2014). It recently dethroned Java as the default coding language at top-ranked US universities, as now eight of the top ten CS departments teach Python in introductory CS courses (Guo, 2014). The three largest MOOC providers (edX, Coursera, and Udacity) all offer introductory programming courses in Python. The language is used by Google, Dropbox, Instagram, Mozilla, and many more companies, and is the de facto standard in data science. Like JavaScript, it has a large and active community. As a conclusion, Python is an often recommended and popular first language for beginners to learn, in combination with either Django or Flask (both are frameworks).

Ruby is a server-side scripting language that was made hugely popular by the Ruby on Rails framework, a full-stack web framework. It is a "very high level language, which means Ruby abstracts away (i.e. handles for you) most of the complex details of the machine. Thus, you can quickly build something from scratch with less lines of code" (Codementor, 2016b). This ease of prototyping makes Ruby a popular choice among tech startups. Its syntax "reads like English" and, when used with Rails, Ruby offers tools that make common development tasks easier "out-of-the-box" (Codementor, 2016b). A very active online community means that there are many great tutorials, documentation, and stack overflow answers available. Well-known sites like Airbnb, GitHub, Twitch.tv, or Shopify have been built with Ruby on Rails. As a conclusion, Ruby is a popular choice for beginners.

PHP is a server-side scripting language that is heavily specialized for the web. It is usually considered beginner-friendly "because it's easier to conceptualize what the PHP code will do, so it's not difficult to pick up" (Codementor, 2016b). There are many popular content management systems using PHP that enable non-technical people to set up their websites or shopping carts with little or no coding required, e.g.

WordPress or Wix. "PHP has a wealth of learning resources, but you should make sure to avoid outdated tutorials" (Codementor, 2016c). Most of the pages on the web are built with PHP, and prominent examples include Facebook, Wikipedia, or Yahoo!. Nonetheless, many programmers agree on that "it seems to be getting less popular" (Sourour, 2016) for a variety of reasons, which is why many people recommend learning full-stack JavaScript, Ruby, or Python instead.

Java is an extremely popular language and can run (almost) anywhere. It is the language used to build Android apps, and can also be used to build desktop applications and web applications (either as a stand-alone backend, or coupled with JSP). It is mature, stable, and there are a many resources available to learn Java. It also is one of the mostly widely taught Object Oriented Programming languages in colleges and universities around the world (Sourour, 2016), even though it has been declining and is being replaced by Python more and more (Guzdial, 2011). After having learned Java, transitioning to other languages is easy. Nonetheless, Java is "designed for larger programs, not beginner programs – the learning curve is steep for the basics of procedural programming" (Figg, 2013). For this reason, it would be a somewhat uncommon choice to pick Java as a first programming language for learning web development.

C is one of the most widely used programming languages. Famous programmer Joel Spolsky once said that C is to programming as learning basic anatomy is to a medical doctor. (Pinola, 2013) summarizes:

> "C is a 'machine level' language, so you'll learn how a program interacts with the hardware and learn the fundamentals of programming at the lowest—hardware—level (C is the foundation for Linux/GNU). You learn things like debugging programs, memory management, and how computers work that you don't get from higher level languages like Java—all while prepping you to code efficiently for other languages. C is the 'grandfather' of many other higher level languages, including Java, C#, and JavaScript. That said, coding in C is stricter and has a steeper learning curve than other languages, and if you're not planning on working on programs that interface with the hardware (tap into device drivers, for example, or operating system extensions), learning C will add to your education time, perhaps unnecessarily".

As a conclusion, C is not as beginner-friendly as other languages, because learners need a long time before being able to build anything useful.

C# is a language created by Microsoft to directly compete with Java. Until recently, it was not well supported on non-Microsoft systems, but that is quickly changing. Like Java, it is object oriented, and can be used to build not only web applications (either as a standalone backend or coupled with ASP.net) but also for desktop apps as well. If you're a Windows user and want a slightly more contained eco-system to program within, C# is your language of choice (Sourour, 2016). Just like C and Java, C# has a sharp learning curve in the beginning, which might not make it the best choice for a beginner that wants to build things on the web.

Lastly, in chapter 2.5, we mentioned the so-called beginner languages like Alice, Kara, and Scratch. While these might be useful in a university setting, it is very unusual for learners who want to learn specific skills in web development to use these languages. They are intended to teach more abstract CS concepts, which are usually picked up through "learning by doing" in the more practical approach followed by self-learners.

Choosing a programming language may seem overwhelming. But as (Trautman, 2015a) points out, it is no use stressing out too much about this decision as "once you learn one language well, it's much easier to jump into another later." Treehouse points out that "as long as you choose a language that is regularly used in technology today, you're winning. When you are starting out, the goal is to become solid in the basics, and the basics are pretty similar across almost all modern programming languages" (Christensen, 2015). Additionally, for projects that are not overly complicated, "most of the 'mainstream' programming languages […] can do the same—or nearly the same—tasks as the others" (Pinola, 2013). In this paper, I recommend choosing either full-stack JavaScript, Python, or Ruby. These seem to be the most widely used and supported languages on the web today. Especially JavaScript and Python are generally believed to become more important in the near future, and Ruby still enjoys widespread popularity in the startup world. Out of the three, JavaScript seems to be the most exciting language to learn today due to frameworks like React which is rapidly gaining in popularity and making JavaScript an even more powerful and versatile programming language.

Lastly, after having picked a language to learn, it is generally recommended to stick with it until you have understood the programming concepts behind it (e.g. data structures or algorithms) (Kim & Harnish, 2012).

3.2.2 Finding effective learning resources

The internet is full of free resources that teach programming. There are interactive tutorials that allow you to code in your browser and give you instant feedback, notable ones being Codecademy and Khan Academy. You can follow MOOCs[6] that are taught by professors from the best universities in the world or by practitioners from tech firms like Google. There are hundreds of programming books on virtually all programming topics you can download for free. There are video tutorials and explanations of programming concepts on YouTube. You can follow blogs where programmers explain hard-to-grasp concepts or walk you through step-by-step tutorials, or listen to dozens of podcasts on programming. "The dilemma comes

---

[6] MOOC stands for 'massive open online course'. The major MOOC platforms are Coursera, Udacity, edX, Udemy, and MITOpenCourseWare

when you're faced with all those reasonable-seeming approaches and need to choose between them or risk wasting your time. The problem, therefore, isn't a lack of resources or even a path, it's a set of criteria for figuring out which path makes the most sense for you to take" (Trautman, 2015a).

Many self-learners are attracted to resources that promise to teach them "how to code" from zero to one, all in one place and from the comfort of their browser. These resources are usually of good quality, but they promise too much, as they actually only one particular skill or language at a time – they do not provide guidance as to which one to learn first, why a specific skill would be useful, and in which order to progress. The following table illustrates this point by providing an overview of the top six available web development courses at four of the most popular programming tutorial sites.

Codecademy	Khan Academy
Make a website	Intro to JS: Drawing & Animation
Make an interactive website	Intro to HTML/CSS: Making webpages
Learn Sass	Intro to SQL: Querying and managing data
Deploy a website	Advanced JS: Games & Visualizations
Learn Ruby on Rails	Advanced JS: Natural Simulations
Learn AngularJS 1.X	HTML/JS: Making webpages interactive

Coursera	Udacity
Web Design for Everybody	Intro to HTML and CSS
Full stack web development	JavaScript Basics
Ruby on Rails web development	Linux Command Line Basics
HTML, CSS, and JavaScript for web developers	How to Use Git and GitHub
Multiplatform Mobile App Development	Intro to Computer Science
Single Page Web Applications with AngularJS	Programming Foundations with Python

Figure 2: Course offering at Codecademy, Khan Academy, Coursera, and Udacity. Retrieved on August 20th 2016.

Even though each of these courses is of great quality, how would learners know which course to take first? Such a curriculum is either unavailable, or you have to pay a lot of money for it (Udacity, for example, offers so-called nanodegrees for $200 per month). For this reason, it is recommended to start with choosing a comprehensive learning curriculum on the web that will guide your learning.

There are several different options, and their structure usually resembles that of coding bootcamps: they provide a clear outline of what to learn and in which order, usually with the aim of getting a job as a software developer. While this may not be your goal, the skills you need to learn to build web applications are the same. No matter if you choose one or several curricula to guide your learning, structuring your approach in such a way is essential. The point is not to stick with one curriculum at all costs, but rather to have an overview of what you are studying. Diving right into tutorials like Codecademy without having a clear order of progression in mind is usually a waste of time – and no one resource like a single interactive tutorial, book, or MOOC will be able to teach you everything you need to know to build a more complex project successfully from scratch. As (Larson, 2016a) notes, there is no "one-stop shop" for learning programming online. "No such thing exists. Certainly not for a field as deep and dynamic as software development". A large-scale survey of more than 15,000 programming self-learners has shown that on average, self-learners use at least three different resources for learning programming (Larson, 2016b).

A popular curriculum to help you structure your learning is called Free Code Camp. It describes itself as "an open source community that helps you learn to code" (Free Code Camp, 2016). Free Code Camp is organized around a core curriculum (called 'map') that learners can follow along. It assumes no prior knowledge of the web or programming. Learners start with a "front-end certification" that involves tutorials on basic HTML, CSS, and JavaScript which are comparable with what Codecademy offers. The difference is that these basics are then quickly complemented by algorithm challenges to improve learners' problem solving skills, and real projects that need to be built based on agile user stories. You are encouraged to research unclear notions on your own, which avoids the excessive handholding of many interactive tutorials and MOOCs, what makes the learning more effective. After having built 10 projects such as a personal portfolio website, and having learned about intermediate JavaScript, JSON, as well as APIs, you can move on to learn data visualization with D3 and React (two JavaScript frameworks), or continue with a back-end certification which will teach you how to build and deploy web applications with Node.js, Express.js, Angular.js, and MongoDB (the 'MEAN stack'). If learners prefer to use different technologies such as React or Ruby on Rails, they are explicitly encouraged to do so – all back-end challenges and projects can be completed "using whichever languages and frameworks you want" (Larson, 2016c). Nonetheless, Free Code Camp advises beginners to "focus 100% of your time on mastering JavaScript" before moving on to other languages.

Free Code Camp has been gaining traction and very favorable reviews for several reasons. First, it is structured as a free open source project, which means there are no paywalls as in many other resources. For example, in order to get better feedback and more guidance on Codecademy, you need to upgrade to 'Pro' for $19.99 a month. Similarly, in all major MOOCs, participation is free. But in order to get the projects reviewed and graded, to get advice on which courses to choose and in what order, and to get a certificate, learners need to pay substantial amounts of money. Second, Free Code Camp is built as a community of self-learners, and thus has an active forum where you can get answers to your questions on projects quickly and for free. Additionally, there are meetups organized in major cities around the world, and students are encouraged to connect with each other and pair program. It also hosts a blog which provides well-written advice that caters to beginners. Third, Free Code Camp follows an open approach and does not try to make learners use their platform exclusively – on the contrary. In many instances, Free Code Camp makes use of existing third-party tutorials when they are of superior quality. Learners are encouraged to try different resources and complement them with each other. This transparent approach has been valued by self-learners. A popular resource that is recommended to complement Free Code Camp is the site 'JavaScript is Sexy', which provides great explanations and also a curriculum which can be found here (http://bit.ly/lrn-code-01).

There are several great alternatives to the Free Code Camp curriculum (which, as seen above, focuses on full-stack JavaScript for its back-end certification). If you want to learn Ruby and Rails instead, you can check out a curriculum called the Odin Project (http://bit.ly/lrn-code-02) that also gets very favorable reviews from self-learners. For Python, a site called Bento.io offers a curriculum that uses Flask as a framework. In case you prefer using Python with Django, a less extensive but nonetheless helpful guide can be found here (http://bit.ly/lrn-code-03). Another, more technical curriculum has been put together by Google here (http://bit.ly/lrn-code-04). aGupieWare has replicated a typical undergraduate computer science university curriculum you can find here (http://bit.ly/lrn-code-05) using only MOOCs that are available for free[7]. With the exception of the more technical approaches mentioned last, these curricula are interchangeable for the front-end part, as all cover HML, CSS, and JavaScript. To complement any of the previously introduced curricula, you can find a helpful blog post on structuring your front-end learning here (http://bit.ly/lrn-code-06 – part 1) and here (http://bit.ly/lrn-code-07 – part 2). As a conclusion, you can pick the curriculum that teaches the back-end language you want to focus on later, and complement it with others for reference and whenever you get stuck. You could also try out several curricula and pick a back-end language based on which one is taught in the curriculum you liked best.

After having chosen a curriculum, learners can complement the suggested resources whenever a concept has not been explained well enough for them to understand it, and whenever they need something which is not covered by their curriculum. "Sometimes hearing a slightly different way of phrasing something can make your mind look at the problem from a different angle and spark understanding" (Oakley, 2014). In general, it helps to remind yourself of the fact that "what you learn through a single teacher or book is a partial version of the full, three-dimensional reality of the subject, which has links to still other fascinating topics that are of your choosing" (Oakley, 2014). To complement your learning, the most notable interactive tutorials are the previously mentioned Codecademy and Khan academy, as well as GA Dash, and Tuts+. They mostly offer individual courses that teach one language or framework at a time. Bento.io provides a helpful curation of learning resources around the web that makes it easier to choose. There are also many

---

[7] Scott H. Young followed this approach and went through the whole MIT computer science undergraduate curriculum in a year's worth of full-time studying, in what he called the 'MIT challenge'.

self-learners who share their experiences with specific resources online – great places to find opinions are the /learnprogramming sub-Reddit, the question-and-answer site Quora, and Stack Overflow. Additionally, a more comprehensive list of resources can be found here (http://bit.ly/lrn-code-08). It includes hundreds of tutorials and learning resources for all current languages and frameworks. If you prefer the more visual approach of MOOCs, a list of close to 1,000 courses by all major providers can be found here (http://bit.ly/lrn-code-09). It also helps with choosing, as it includes a rating system.

When having trouble understanding new concepts, you can also refer to programming books. Books are usually well-written and structured, which is great for more challenging topics. Additionally, they cover topics in a deeper way than other resources, which usually guarantees you have a good understanding of what you are learning. You can find curated lists of free programming books here (http://bit.ly/lrn-code-10) and here (http://bit.ly/lrn-code-11) – they include the "standard" books that most people recommend. Additionally, you can find a comprehensive collection of more than 500 high-quality, free books here (http://bit.ly/lrn-code-12) that offers even more choice. The visual alternative to books is YouTube videos, which tend to be shorter and more concise. Being able to see people coding while listening to the explanation can be of great help, and some channels are of outstanding quality. Here (http://bit.ly/lrn-code-13) is a great list of 33 YouTube channels for programmers, including which languages and frameworks are covered. While this is certainly no academic observation, all useful YouTube tutorials I have ever used personally are included in this list. For learning 'on the go', programming podcasts can be useful. Curated collections that are geared towards beginners can be found here (http://bit.ly/lrn-code-14), here (http://bit.ly/lrn-code-15), and here (http://bit.ly/lrn-code-16).

As a general rule, you should keep in mind that the most important criterion for evaluating whether to choose one resource over another is to determine if it matches your learning style. It helps to answer the simple question: "how do I enjoy learning the most (i.e. which type of resources)?" (Trautman, 2015a). Especially when starting out in the beginning, you should "start by trying out different resources to find how you learn best and what sorts of projects are the most interesting to you. Maybe it's Khan Academy's quick challenges, Codecademy's in-browser exercises, Chris Pine's Learn to Program book or Code School's wacky try Ruby experience. Be open minded at the start" (Trautman, 2015b). At the same time, some resources like MOOCs can be valuable to grasp a single concept, but finishing them just for the sake of finishing can be a waste of time. "You need to dig deeper than the marketing slogans and smiling faces on course websites or book jackets to ask 'will this help me accomplish the goal I've set or not?'" (Trautman, 2015b).

As a conclusion, you should always stay focused on your initial learning goal, i.e. what you want to achieve with learning programming. "When you focus on what you want to do versus what class to take next, you subtly shift your mindset from one that is skills-based to one that is competency-based" (Akiko, 2015). What counts is not to earn another badge on Codecademy, it is to make progress towards your learning goal. All the online resources are simply a means to an end, and should always be regarded as such.

3.3 Optimizing the learning

This paper would be incomplete without introducing effective learning strategies – "successful learning in every learning environment involves the use of effective learning strategies" (Song & Hill, 2007). The following section starts with introducing actionable learning techniques to make learning more effective that have come out of psychological research on learning (3.3.1). Afterwards, I underline the importance of 'learning by doing' in programming – a recommendation which is widely accepted by academics as well as among practitioners (3.3.2). Lastly, the section concludes with advice from expert programmers and other self-learners that is intended to guide your learning and avoid mistakes that others have done before you (3.3.3).

3.3.1 Actionable takeaways from learning research

Psychological research in the past few decades has come up with a host of techniques which make learning more efficient. And "these approaches aren't get-smarter schemes that require computer software, gadgets, or medication. Nor are they based on any grand teaching philosophy, intended to lift the performance of entire classrooms. On the contrary, they are small alterations, alterations in how we study or practice that we can apply individually, in our own lives, right now" (Carey, 2014). These learning techniques help learners to make the best use of their limited study time, which is essential when learning programming is not your full-time job. "It is not that there is a right way and wrong way to learn. It's that there are different strategies, each uniquely suited to capturing a particular type of information" (Carey, 2014). The following section introduces the techniques that are most relevant for self-learners of programming – first for problem solving and understanding new concepts (3.3.1.1), then for increasing retention of newly learned material (3.3.1.2), and lastly to deal with procrastination (3.3.1.3).

3.3.1.1 Problem solving strategies and how to understand difficult programming concepts

A key finding from neuroscience is that the human brain switches between two different types of thinking processes: the focused mode, and the diffuse mode. Focused-mode thinking "involves a direct approach to solving problems using rational, sequential, analytical approaches" (Oakley, 2014). When learners concentrate on a problem they are trying to solve, they are in focused mode. Diffuse mode thinking, on the other hand, "is what happens when you relax your attention and just let your mind wander. [...] It is associated with 'big-picture' perspectives" (Oakley, 2014). Shifting from focused to diffused mode happens naturally when we distract ourselves from a problem at hand and allow some time to pass. You can go for a walk, take a shower, nap for a bit, or go to the gym – any activity you find relaxing and that activates other parts of your brain. "The key is to do something else until your brain is consciously free of any thought of the problem" (Oakley, 2014) or concept you are studying. How does this relate to problem-solving? Switching between both modes of thinking is helpful and essential for solving problems:

> "Once you are distracted from the problem at hand, the diffuse mode has access and can begin pinging about in its big-picture way to settle on a solution. [...] When you return to the problem at hand, you will often be surprised at how easily the solution pops into place. Even if the solution doesn't appear, you will often be further along in your understanding. It can take a lot of hard focused-mode thinking beforehand, but the sudden, unexpected solution that emerges from the diffuse mode can make it feel almost like the 'aha!' mode" (Oakley, 2014).

In order to take advantage of this shifting between focused and diffuse mode when solving problems or trying to understand new concepts, you should take regular breaks, especially when you get stuck: "your best bet is to turn off your precision-focused thinking and turn on your 'big-picture' diffuse mode, long enough to be able to latch on to a new, more fruitful approach" (Oakley, 2014). She then quotes Shaun Wassell, a freshman in computer science: "The harder you push your brain to come up with something creative, the less creative your ideas will be. [...] Ultimately, this means that relaxation is an important part of hard work – and good work, for that matter". Nonetheless, research has clearly shown that people do not benefit from taking breaks "unless they have reached an impasse" (Carey, 2014). "Just using your diffuse mode doesn't mean you can lollygag around and expect to get anywhere. As the days and weeks pass, it's the distributed practice – the back and forth between focused-mode attention and diffuse-mode relaxation – that does the trick" (Oakley, 2014). Additionally, learners should keep in mind that when learning new concepts, a good rule of thumb seems to be "not to let things go untouched for longer than a day" (Oakley, 2014).

In the same vein as taking regular breaks, getting enough sleep makes a remarkable difference in learners' ability to solve problems and find meaning and understanding in what they are learning. It can be especially hard for self-learners as "for many of you, you have to balance your coding schedules on top of your busy work and family responsibilities" (Mayeux, 2016). Nonetheless, it is essential to get enough sleep – research has shown that "sleep improves retention and comprehension of what was studied the day before" (Carey, 2014). The Russian scientist Dmitri Mendeleev "reportedly pulled several all-nighters, to no avail, trying to piece together what would become his famous periodic table of the elements, but it was only after nodding off, he told a colleague, that he saw 'a table where all the elements fell into place'" (Carey, 2014). An actionable technique for learners is to go over difficult material "right before taking a nap or going to sleep for the evening, [as] you will have an increased chance of dreaming about it. [...] Dreaming about what you are studying can substantially enhance your ability to understand. [...] If you're tired, it's often best to just go to sleep and get up a little earlier the next day" (Oakley, 2014).

Another insight that came from studying the human brain is that in order to progress in your learning, you need to "create conceptual chunks – mental leaps that unite separate bits of information through meaning." (Oakley, 2014). Chunking has been defined by psychologists as a process by which individual pieces of information are bound together into a meaningful whole (Surprenant & Neath, 2013). A more tangible explanation comes from (Miller, 1956): "A man just beginning to learn radio-telegraphic code hears each dit and dah as a separate chunk. Soon he is able to organize these sounds into letters and then he can deal with the letters as chunks. Then the letters organize themselves as words, which are still larger chunks, and he begins to hear whole phrases". Another example is that instead of remembering strings of letters such as "Y-M-C-A-I-B-M-D-H-L", it is easier to remember the chunks "YMCA-IBM-DHL" consisting of the same letters – your brain needs to encode only three items as opposed to ten in the non-chunked version. We've all used chunking when learning new concepts before, most obviously when learning letters in our native language as young children. The main benefit of chunking new information is that it "helps your brain run more efficiently. Once you chunk an idea or concept, you don't need to remember all the little underlying details" (Oakley, 2014), and your short-term memory is free to focus on more advanced aspects of what you are trying to achieve. Building a chunked library of concepts also helps you "build intuition in problem solving" (Oakley, 2014). In short, chunking facilitates comprehension and retrieval of learning materials.

When you want to chunk a programming concept or problem solving strategy, the first step is to "simply focus your attention on the information you want to chunk. [...] The second step [...] is to understand the basic idea you are trying to chunk. [...] The third step to chunking is gaining context so you see not just how, but also when to use this chunk. Context means going beyond the initial problem and seeing more broadly, practicing with both related and unrelated problems so you see not only when to use the chunk, but when not to use it." (Oakley, 2014). Simply "understanding what's going on is not usually enough to create a chunk".

Apart from the main insights that were just introduced, learning research has come up with several other actionable techniques which build on the insights of diffuse and focused thinking, and that are easy to implement in your study routine.

Embrace failure. "Analyze what you did wrong and use it to correct yourself to do better in the future. Failures are better teachers than successes because they cause you to rethink your approach" (Oakley, 2014). Learners should keep in mind that "we learn a good deal from our failures. [...] Know that you are making progress with each mistake you catch when trying to solve a problem – finding errors should give you a sense of satisfaction. Edison [...] is said to have noted 'I have not failed. I've just found 10,000 ways that won't work.'" (Oakley, 2014).

Avoid Einstellung. Focused attention can often help solve problems, but it can also block learners' ability to see new solutions: "Accepting the first idea that comes to mind [...] can prevent you from finding a better solution" (Oakley, 2014), a phenomenon called Einstellung (the German word for mindset). Here is a short example, taken from (Oakley, 2014). In the figure below, you are given two triangles to put together into a square shape, and it's easy to do, as shown on the left. If you are given two more triangles and told to form a square, your first tendency is to erroneously put them together to form a rectangle, as shown in the middle. This is because you've already laid down a focused-mode pattern that you have a tendency to follow. It takes an intuitive, diffuse leap to realize that you need to completely rearrange the pieces if you want to form another square, as shown on the right. In order to prevent Einstellung, it can be helpful to take a break to activate your diffuse mode of thinking which allows you to be more creative and 'think out of the box'.

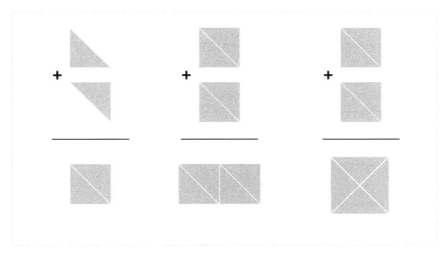

Figure 3: Avoiding Einstellung when solving problems

Interleaving problems is important. When learning a new problem-solving approach or concept, learners tend to "learn the new technique and then practice it over and over again during the same study session. Continuing the study or practice after it is well understood is called overlearning. Overlearning can have its place – it can help produce an automaticity that is important when you are executing a serve in tennis or

36

playing a perfect piano concerto. But be wary of repetitive overlearning during a single session […] – research has shown it can be a waste of valuable learning time". Overlearning is common because "it's easy and it feels good to successfully solve problems" (Oakley, 2014). Additionally, "if the homework says 'The Quadratic Formula' at the top of the page, you just use that blindly. There's no need to ask whether it's appropriate" (Carey, 2014), which means you lack the understanding of when to use a new method, and what kinds of other problems it can solve. To avoid these issues, learners should interleave their practice: "interleaving means practice by doing a mixture of different kinds of problems requiring different strategies". While it can sometimes "seem to make your learning more difficult", interleaving is important because "it helps you learn more deeply" (Oakley, 2014). Unfortunately, most online tutorials (e.g. Codecademy, w3schools, and many MOOCs) have the problem described above: they introduce a concept or method, and quiz learners right away – you already know which method to apply before doing the problem. Self-learners should thus try to mix methods as much as possible and also practice on sites where there are no headings that give away the method to be used (examples provided in 3.3.2). "Mixed problem sets […] not only remind you what you've learned but also trains you to match the problem types with the appropriate strategies" (Carey, 2014).

Use metaphors and analogies. One of the best ways to understand new programming concepts is to create a metaphor or analogy for it. "A metaphor is just a way of realizing that one thing is somehow similar to another. […] If you're trying to understand electrical current, it can help to visualize it as water. Similarly, electrical voltage can 'feel like' pressure. Voltage helps push the electrical current to where you want it to go, just like a mechanical pump uses physical pressure to push real water" (Oakley, 2014). There are many examples of using metaphors in programming, e.g. using animals or cars to explain object oriented programming. Then, "as you climb to a more sophisticated understanding of […] whatever topic you are concentrating on, you can revise your metaphors, or toss them away and create more meaningful ones" (Oakley, 2014).

Explain new concepts in simple terms. You can try to explain a new concept in simple terms to yourself (e.g. by writing a blog about your learning) or others. Doing so helps with understanding and retaining new information. "Surprisingly, simple explanations are possible for almost any concept, no matter how complex. When you cultivate simple explanations by breaking down complicated material to its key elements, the result is that you have a deeper understanding of the material. […] You'll be surprised to see how often understanding arises as a consequence of attempts to explain to others and yourself, rather than the explanation arising out of your previous understanding" (Oakley, 2014). "These apparently simple attempts to communicate what you've learned […] are not merely a form of self-testing, in the conventional sense, but studying – the high-octane kind, 20 to 30 percent more powerful than if you continued sitting on your butt, staring at that outline. [...] They'll expose what you don't know, where you're confused, what you've forgotten" (Carey, 2014). In the same spirit, an interesting place to check out is the Reddit 'explain like I'm five' which also includes some explanations of programming concepts.

3.3.1.2 Improving the retention of newly learned material

In order to learn and retain new information, many people – according to a survey conducted by (Weimer, 2014), as much as to 80% – make use of re-reading, i.e. they read the same passage over and over to make it stick. Unfortunately, psychologists have found that "when you have the book (or Google!) open right in front of you, it provides the illusion that the material is also in your brain. *But it's not.* Because it can be easier to look at the book instead of recalling, students persist in their illusion – studying in a far less productive way" (Oakley, 2014). This is called an illusion of competence, and is a common pitfall for leaners. For this reason, while re-reading is an intuitive and commonly used way of studying, it is "labor in vain – students are putting in labor but not getting anywhere". "Unless you can prove that the material is moving into your brain by recalling the main ideas without looking at the page, re-reading is a waste of time" (Oakley, 2014). (Kim & Harnish, 2012) confirm that illusions of competence are a common mistake of people that are learning how to program: "Having solved one set of problem doesn't mean that you will remember that programming solution you created next time when you have to solve a similar problem."

Instead of re-reading, after you read a page, try to recall as much of the information as you can. Research published in the journal Science has shown that "in the same amount of time, by simply practicing and recalling the material, students learned far more and at a much deeper level than they did using any other approach, including simply re-reading the text a number of times or drawing concept maps that supposedly enriched the relationships in the materials under study" (Oakley, 2014). There's an additional benefit: "it also shows you immediately what you don't know and need to circle back and review" (Carey, 2014).

Unfortunately, many of the most popular learning resources teach programming in a way that closely resembles re-reading. Codecademy, which is now used by as many as 16 million people (Lunden & Shieber, 2016), introduces new concepts by prompting students to repeat them right away. Other programming tutorials follow a similar approach.

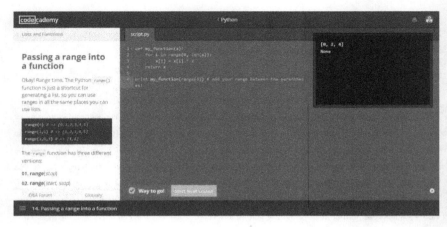

Figure 4: Screenshot from a Codecademy tutorial

Learners complete a lesson by repeating what they just read in the browser, earn a badge for completing the challenge, and then scarcely revisit the material ever again. This makes many programming tutorials appear like simple interactive walkthroughs of language syntax documentation, and leads to many concepts being forgotten after a short time: "the easier it is to call a fact to mind, the smaller the increase in learning" (Carey, 2014). (Mayeux, 2016) describes his experience: "[I] started off with some tutorials on Codecademy, and followed along with the instructional prompts, only to feel 'stuck' and unable to produce a website from scratch without copying and pasting. I had probably gone through their JavaScript tutorials three times, and I still felt like I wasn't learning anything". Self-learners should therefore avoid relying exclusively on learning resources that make use of passive learning strategies like repeating new concepts right away:

> "Most of the examples will appear simple and straightforward. But there is a big difference between reading through a code example and being actually able to write the code on your own and to run it successfully. If you read through programming tutorials and books without actually doing the hands-on examples on your own, you won't get much benefit out of your investment" (Kim & Harnish, 2012).

This is not to say that Codecademy and similar tutorials are bad – but using them without complementing your learning with recall and additional resources is an ineffective way of studying. Next to recalling new concepts in your mind, another established way of improving the retention of new information is to actively take notes and review them with a technique called spaced repetition.

Spaced repetition is "a learning technique that incorporates increasing intervals of time between subsequent review of previously learned material" (Wikipedia, 2016e). This means that you review the new concepts in your notes at gradually increasing intervals. It is based on the insight that for a new fact to move into your long-term memory, "two things should happen: the idea should be memorable, and it must be repeated" (Oakley, 2014). Otherwise, the new information will be forgotten[8]. As a matter of fact, research has shown "there is an ideal moment to practice what you've learned. Practice too soon and you waste your time. Practice too late and you've forgotten the material and have to relearn it. The right time to practice is just at the moment you're about to forget" (Wolf, 2008). This intuition is based on one of the most powerful findings that came out of learning research: the spacing effect, which is defined as "the phenomenon whereby learning is greater when studying is spread out over time, as opposed to studying the same amount of time in a single session" (Wikipedia, 2016f). In other words, "people learn at least as much, and retain it much longer, when they distribute – or 'space' – their study time than when they concentrate it". Additionally, "repeating facts right after you've studied them gives you nothing, no added memory benefit". (Carey, 2014). As a conclusion, in order to commit a new fact to memory, you should space out the repetitions to improve retention.

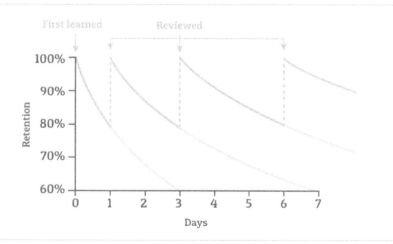

Figure 5: The forgetting curve – source: (Wranx, 2016)

---

[8] This forgetting is actually a useful, natural metabolic process of the human brain. As (Oakley, 2014) points out, "much of what goes on around you is basically trivial – if you remembered it all, you'd end up like a hoarder, trapped in an immense collection of useless memories".

A common and practical way of implementing spaced repetition in a learning routine is by using a software like Anki (which is free to use and open source). The learner creates a system of flashcards, where the items to be memorized are entered as question-answer pairs. The software then uses an algorithm to show the flashcards to the learner at the optimal point in time. When this approach is used daily, learners can "remember thousands of these facts in only 20 minutes a day" (Sievers, 2013) with a bit of practice. (Sievers, 2013) also recommends making the practice a daily routine, e.g. in the morning: "Make a cup of boiling tea. Do my Anki. Drink my tea".

The creator of the first software method using the spaced repetition technique, (Wozniak, 1999), gives recommendations on how to formulate effective flash cards. First, he notes that before trying to memorize a concept, learners need to have understood it. This means avoiding "blind learning" of facts that have not yet been understood, and "building an overall picture of the learned knowledge" instead of trying to learn isolated pieces of knowledge. Second, he recommends to "build upon the basics" and use simple items. When an item is too complicated, it should be split up into smaller chunks. These are the first four of twenty rules that Wozniak has deemed to be bringing "most benefit if complied with" – his original article is well worth a read for the complete list. As a conclusion, space based repetition is a highly effective learning technique that has its place in learning programming. (Sievers, 2013) calls it "the most helpful learning technique [he] ever encountered in 14 years of computer programming".

As a side note, when using the term 'memorization', this paper does not mean memorizing simple facts such as specific function names or parameter lists – this kind of knowledge can be looked up on the internet easily. "You don't have to remember all of the semantic HTML5 tags or all of the Bootstrap classes to make a website. Why would you have to do that when you could just find whatever you need in the API docs, Google, or Stack Overflow? In my very early days of learning HTML and CSS, I actually made flashcards to help me remember this stuff, and I can't believe what a waste of time it was" (Mayeux, 2016). What is meant by 'memorization' is to build an active vocabulary of keywords and concepts that are *useful for solving problems* and that learners can access fluently: "repeating what one has succeeded at and expanding on that knowledge will lead to a stronger foundation for more advanced programming knowledge" (Kim & Harnish, 2012). For example, when learning JavaScript, learners need to memorize different ways of manipulating arrays –they need to know that a certain method like Array.prototype.sort exists before being able to search for it on Google. And before knowing how to manipulate an array, they need to know what the concept of array means – it would be incredibly inefficient to look up such a common term on the internet every time. On top of that, research has shown that "having more facts on board could very well help with comprehension, too" (Carey, 2014): memorizing small chunks of information "in your long-term memory helps gradually build your big-picture understanding of a subject" (Oakley, 2014). The relationship between memorization and understanding goes both ways: "the most important part of your memorization practices is to understand what the [material] really means. Understanding also helps a lot with the memorization process" (Oakley, 2014).

3.3.1.3 Avoiding procrastination

As the spacing effect shows, it is better to study regularly than to put in irregular, long cramming sessions. "Breaking up study or practice time – dividing it into two or three sessions, instead of one – is far more effective than concentrating it". The more sessions, the better, "as long as you're giving yourself enough time to dive into the material each time" (Carey, 2014). However, this strategy is of no use if instead of starting to study, you procrastinate and spend half an hour browsing on Facebook. More learning sessions mean that you need to force yourself to start studying many more times – you need to master procrastination to learn effectively.

When learning programming, self-learners will inevitably struggle with hard-to-grasp and dry concepts – "it's easy to feel distaste for something you're not good at" (Oakley, 2014) – and people procrastinate about things that make them feel uncomfortable. Neuroscientists have shown that people who dislike math, for example, "appear to avoid math because even just thinking about it seems to hurt. The pain centers of their brains light up when they contemplate working on math" (Oakley, 2014). Procrastination is about avoiding these things that make us feel bad momentarily, and replacing them with things that make us feel comfortable (like Twitter, YouTube cat videos or your Facebook timeline). And unfortunately, "what makes us feel good temporarily isn't necessarily good for us in the long run" (Oakley, 2014).

Interestingly, though, the same neuroscientists who found that thinking about math caused pain for some people also found "it was the anticipation that was painful. When the mathphobes actually did math, the pain disappeared. [...] The dread of doing a task uses up more time and energy than doing the task itself" (Oakley, 2014). This finding is used to suggest a strategy for mastering procrastination:

> "Learn to focus on process, not product. Process means the flow of time and the habits and actions associated with that flow of time – as in, 'I'm going to spend twenty minutes working'. Product is an outcome – for example, a homework assignment that you need to finish. To prevent procrastination, you want to avoid concentrating on product. Instead, your attention should be on building processes – habits – that allow you to do the unpleasant tasks that need to be done. [...] Who cares whether you finished the homework or grasped key concepts in any one session? The whole point instead is that you calmly put forth your best effort for a short period – the process" (Oakley, 2014).

A common way to put this into practice is by using the Pomodoro technique. The methodology is simple: you break down your work "into short, timed intervals (called 'Pomodoros') that are spaced out by short breaks" (Henry, 2014). The length of a single Pomodoro is typically 25 minutes, complemented with five minute breaks. Nonetheless, some people prefer longer intervals, and the length can be adapted to individual preferences. The advantage of Pomodoro is that "you work in short sprints, which makes sure you're consistently productive. You also get to take regular breaks that bolster your motivation and keep you creative" (Henry, 2014). It is important to ignore distractions while doing a Pomodoro. Commonly used techniques are to put your phone into flight mode, open a fresh browser window to work in, and put yourself in a quiet space or use noise-cancelling headphones. It is simple to use the Pomodoro technique: all you need is a timer which can easily be found online. The key take-away is to "just get started", avoid distractions, and take regular breaks.

Another common way of dealing with procrastination is to set goals for yourself regularly. (Oakley, 2014) describes the approach as follows: "for the next two weeks, write your weekly goals down at the beginning of each week. Then, each day, write out five to ten small, reasonable daily goals based on your weekly goals. Cross off each item as you complete it, and mentally savor each completed item that you cross off your list. If you need to, break a given task into a 'mini task list' of three small subtasks to help keep yourself motivated". Some people recommend doing "the most important and most disliked jobs first", if possible "as soon as you wake up". Additionally, according to (Oakley, 2014), "planning your quitting time is as important as planning your working time". This means that before every study session, learners should have a list of tasks they want to achieve, and also set themselves a time when they will stop.

For larger projects like building a personal portfolio website, self-learners often have the tendency to procrastinate on them and take care of smaller stuff first – doing easy reading, or checking some other things off their to-do-list. Learning research has shown this to be the wrong approach: it is better to start work on the project as early as possible. "The act of starting work on an assignment often gives that job the psychological weight of a goal" (Carey, 2014). Doing so is important because "having a goal foremost in mind tunes our perceptions to fulfilling it. And that tuning determines, to some extent, where we look and what we notice" – a phenomenon called tuned perception. The following paragraph explains how learners can use tuned perception to their advantage:

> "What does this have to do with finishing a research paper on, say, the Emancipation Proclamation? Everything, actually. [...] When we're in the middle of that paper, for example, we're far more attuned to race references all around us. A story about race riots or affirmative action in the media. An offhand comment by a friend. A review of a Lincoln biography in the newspaper. Even the way people of different races arrange themselves at a bar, or on a subway car" (BC p. 142).

It is easy to see how tuned perception applies to longer-term programming projects like for example of building a personal portfolio website: you notice a nice animation on a random website and realize it would fit well on your own website, and save the code for later. Reading blogs or listening to podcasts about programming, or going to code conferences can be of even greater help when your perception is tuned. And as seen before, as soon as you stall with the project, interrupt yourself, take a break, and return to it later.

> "Interrupting yourself when absorbed in an assignment extends its life in memory and […] pushes it to the top of your mental to-do-list. Most interruptions are annoying – especially if it's a busybody neighbor, or the cat needing to be let out, or a telemarketer calling when you're in the middle of an important work assignment. But deliberate self-interruption is something else altogether. It's what […] creates suspense and […] pushes the unfinished […] project to the top of our minds, leaving us to wonder what comes next. Which is exactly where we want it to be if we're working on something long-term and demanding" (Carey, 2014).

As a conclusion, mastering procrastination is essential for self-learners. Most academic researchers and programmers alike agree on the fact that one of the hardest parts of learning programming is keeping up motivation and being persistent – procrastination is the worst enemy of that goal. If you struggle a lot with procrastination, a helpful resource to dig deeper is a free MOOC called "learning how to learn" that is available on Coursera[9]. In short, "it's normal to sit down with a few negative feelings about beginning your work. It's how you handle those feelings that matters" (Oakley, 2014).

3.3.2 The importance of programming practice and building projects

(Norvig, 2001), who is director of research at Google, states that "the best kind of learning is learning by doing". In order to become good at programming, "the key is deliberate practice: not just doing it again and again, but challenging yourself with a task that is just beyond your current ability, trying it, analyzing your performance while and after doing it, and correcting any mistakes. Then repeat. And repeat again." This deliberate practice "requires a well-defined task with an appropriate difficulty level for the particular individual, informative feedback, and opportunities for repetition and corrections of errors". When recommending this, he builds on seminal research by (Ericsson, Krampe, & Tesch-Romer, 1993), who showed that becoming good at a skill has more to do with how one practices than with merely performing a skill many times. The key is to continually practice at more challenging levels – "effortful activities designed to optimize improvement". In other words, deliberate practice means "constantly pushing oneself beyond one's comfort zone, following training activities designed by an expert to develop specific abilities, and using feedback to identify weaknesses and work on them" (Ericsson & Pool, 2016).

---

[9] It is strongly based on and taught by (Oakley, 2014).

Deliberate practice is a highly effective way of learning specific programming techniques, the most common one being how to write algorithms. In computer science, an algorithm is "a set of steps for a computer program to accomplish a task. A good algorithm solves a problem and does so efficiently" (Khan Academy, 2016). Algorithms are used to manipulate arrays that store data, validate data that users provide in web forms, and much more – it is essential to learn about them when learning programming. There are several resources available online that provide a good environment for deliberate practice. First, Free Code Camp has hours worth of algorithm challenges that are very well attuned to beginners and gradually increase in difficulty – find them here (http://bit.ly/lrn-code-17). Codewars, Hackerrank, and Coderbyte are three great websites that also provide a host of practice problems with solutions. Codewars has the advantage of allowing you to compare your solution with that of others, which helps with improving your coding style and can be truly 'eye-opening'. More comprehensive lists of where you can practice can be found here (http://bit.ly/lrn-code-18) and here (http://bit.ly/lrn-code-19). In order to practice your problem-solving skills, a more theoretical approach that is recommended by some programmers can be found in a book called "Structure and Interpretation of Computer Programs", which is available online for free.

It is important to note that practice problems naturally include a solution, and it is tempting for learners to look at the solution and reproduce it. But "merely glancing at the solution to a problem and thinking you know it yourself is one of the most common illusions of competence in learning" (Oakley, 2014). It should be avoided, as solving the problem on your own "forces you to think your way through a problem and provides a self-test of your understanding". You should also keep in mind that practice without conceptual knowledge will hinder further learning progress. "It is hard to learn one without the other, and either of them can become an obstacle that hinders further learning" (Eckerdal, 2009). Lastly, "solving a problem is a good way to learn, but doing so on a regular basis as often as possible is the best way to make what you learned stick and stay in your head" (Kim & Harnish, 2012).

While research on deliberate practice has proven that the approach is highly effective in sports and music, there is a caveat when applying it to programming. Deliberate practice will help you with getting better at specific skills like algorithms, but developing software involves much more than that. The actual amount of time you will spend worrying about efficient algorithms is small when compared to all the rest – figuring out how some tool works for the first time, or getting an API call to work (Tanzer, 2012). As a conclusion, deliberately practicing algorithms is important for beginners in order to establish basic knowledge in the language of your choice, and it should also remain an integral part of your study routine later on to keep improving specific skills. Nonetheless, the most recommended method of studying that should quickly take up most of your time is to build real projects – these are also why you started to learn programming in the first place.

"Computer science education cannot make anybody an expert programmer any more than studying brushes and pigment can make somebody an expert painter", says well-known programmer Eric Raymond (Norvig, 2001), and many self-learners and programmers agree with this view:

> "Coding is a lot like riding a bike, until you put down the books, the tutorials, and actually start doing it, it's very hard for things to "click." Even after you get on the bike and start pedaling, it takes a long time before it feels natural. The same thing goes with learning to programming: start building stuff, start early, keep doing it. I built things. It didn't matter if I didn't know how – the whole point was to build something that I wanted to, and then figure out how to do it along the way. It was the best way to practice and grow my skills" (Chan, 2014).

Many authors emphasize the fact that you should not wait long before starting to build real projects:

> "One of the greatest mistakes in learning programming is putting off writing one's own code and waiting to work on a real-life problem for the reason that one doesn't know yet enough to do so. While it is easy to think that once you learn a bit more, it would be easier to approach a problem, this is actually a counterproductive learning strategy as far as programming is concerned, because often the only way to find out what to learn is by trying to solve a problem" (Kim & Harnish, 2012).

Nonetheless, there are two caveats to consider when building projects. First, your early projects should not be overly ambitious. "Start small and build constantly. You should have interesting big projects in mind for the future, but you'll need to get comfortable debugging and searching for resources with bite-sized challenges" (Trautman, 2015b). (Young, 2012) adds that "it should be short. Don't try to make a new Facebook, since you probably won't finish and most your time will be doing repeat tasks rather than learning". (Sourour, 2016) writes that starting with smaller projects first helps you stay motivated through the feeling of finishing them, and provides you with a "better understanding of how to structure a bigger project". The second caveat is that you should make sure to understand some of the most important concepts needed to succeed in a project *before* starting – otherwise, the project might be overwhelming and you will lose your motivation. "Jumping in the water before [learning] to swim [...] is a recipe for sinking" (Oakley, 2014).

When it comes to choosing project ideas, the curricula of Free Code Camp and Odin Project both have a wealth of recommendations (see figure 6 below). These can be helpful especially for beginners, as the relevant concepts for building the project are introduced in parallel. Additionally, the projects are thoughtfully designed by experts to be hard, but manageable – the definition of good deliberate practice. If you want to build projects with real-life applications, another good resource for inspiration called "Automate the Boring Stuff" can be found here (http://bit.ly/lrn-code-20). It teaches how to use Python to write small programs to automate common every-day tasks like renaming files or manipulating PDF files.

Alternatively, self-taught programmer Jennifer deWalt has published a personal challenge of her own that consisted of building 180 small projects, one every day. You can use these projects as inspiration for what you could build yourself. They can be found here (http://bit.ly/lrn-code-21).

Front-end (basic & intermediate)	Front-end (advanced)	Back-end (API projects)	Dynamic web application projects
Tribute page	JavaScript calculator	Timestamp microservice	Voting app
Personal portfolio page	Pomodoro clock	Request header parser	Nightlife coordination app
Random quote machine	Tic Tac Toe game	URL shortener	Chart the stock market
Local weather app	Simon game	Image abstraction layer	Book trading club
Wikipedia viewer		File metadata microservice	Pinterest clone
Twitch.tv viewer			

Figure 6: Free Code Camp's suggested programming projects

Next to building your own projects, you can also contribute to open source projects. There are thousands of projects on GitHub that have open issues (bugs) you can help to fix. Beginners are often encouraged to contribute as well, which means you can get started even with little experience. Open source projects are a good opportunity to train your "ability to work with others [by having] a contribution reviewed and accepted", and let you write real-life, "actual code" (Mullenweg, 2016). In order to find interesting projects, you can browse through the "showcases" section of GitHub, or use Code Triage which lets you pick your favorite project and will send you a different open issue to your inbox every day. Another way of contributing and finding software to play around with is the Free Software Foundation, which lists all major free software packages like Linux, the MySQL database, the Apache web server, and many more.

Aside from building projects, what many programmers recommend to improve your skills is to read and analyze other people's code. Athletes watch videos of practice sessions and performances. Chess players study games played by grand masters and try to determine what the next move would be. Every time they are wrong, they analyze why – the equivalent in programming is to read other people's code. What was the other programmer thinking? What caused him to choose this approach over another one? What are the trade-offs? Case studies are about observations, analysis, and critical thinking. (Owens, 2013). You can use the above-mentioned showcases section of GitHub to find quality code to study. An alternative is Codepen, where people upload projects they have done and you can see the live result next to the source code. Instead of reading, you can also watch other people code live on Twitch.tv or YouTube.

3.3.3 Advice from expert programmers and other self-learners

This last section provides advice from expert programmers and self-learners that succeeded in learning programming on their own. It is intended to complement the previous chapters and help you avoid mistakes others have done before you. The advice has been collected from online blogs, and consolidated into three main recommendations: you should be persistent as learning programming takes time, you should not be intimidated by 'genius' programmers, and you should get used to debugging.

BE PERSISTENT: LEARNING PROGRAMMING TAKES TIME

"The most important thing to keep in mind is that learning how to program (or how to do anything at all, really) is not going to be an overnight task. Do not be tricked into thinking it will be easy" (Buck, 2011). In the same vein, (Norvig, 2001) wrote an influential blog post with the self-explanatory title "Teach yourself programming in ten years". He warns learners not to be impatient and expect too much too soon. "There appear to be no real shortcuts". (Larson, 2016a) adds that courses promising "everything you need" or "teach yourself C++ in 21 days" just want to cash in on peoples' "impatience and naivety".

Figure 7 was removed for publication as its CC-BY-NC 3.0 US License is incompatible with a commercial publication. It originally showed the Comic #249 "How to Teach Yourself Programming" from Abstruse Goose (http://abstrusegoose.com/249)

The Comic mocks the concept of learning C++ in 21 days by showing a programmer spending a long time to learn programming as well as theoretical physics and biochemistry in order to reverse his aging process, go back in time and then kill and replace his younger, less experienced self on day 21. It concludes with the remark "As far as I know, this is the easiest way to "Teach Yourself C++ in 21 Days"."

Figure 7: Teach yourself C++ in 21 days. Source: http://abstrusegoose.com/249

As a conclusion, you should keep in mind that learning programming is a long journey which takes time, and that the key to success is to persevere. "If you keep putting bricks on top of each other, it might take a long time but eventually you'll have a wall. [...] If you believe that with time and patience you can figure the whole coding thing out, in time you almost certainly will" (Carver, 2013).

DON'T BE INTIMIDATED

Many beginners are intimidated by the sheer amount of knowledge they have to master. The blog posts and tutorials on programming they encounter are often written in a very technical style, which makes them feel outright stupid when comparing themselves with expert programmers. These feelings can be exacerbated after reading blog posts on just how difficult programming is – contributions like the evocatively titled "Please Don't Learn to Code" by (Atwood, 2012) – which (Kaplan-Moss, 2015) calls "the myth of the 'genius programmer': [...] if you don't "rock" at programming, then basically, you suck". (Carver, 2013) provides great advice for learners to overcome this kind of feelings:

> "Coding is a skill like any other. Like language learning, there's grammar and vocabulary to acquire. Like math, there are processes to work through specific types of problems. Like all kinds of craftsmanship and art-making, there are techniques and tools and best practices that people have developed over time, specialized to different tasks, that you're free to use or modify or discard. There's no point in being intimidated or wondering if you're smart enough. Sure, the more complex and esoteric your task, the higher the level of mastery you will need to complete it. But this is true in absolutely every other field. Unless you're planning to make your living entirely by your code, chances are you don't have to be a recursion-understanding genius to make the thing you want to make."

The previously mentioned Jacob Kaplan-Moss, who co-created Django (the Python framework) and is now director of security at Heroku, summarizes and encourages learners: "Programming is just a bunch of skills that can be learned, it doesn't require that much talent, and it's not shameful to be a mediocre programmer".

DON'T BE DISCOURAGED BY HAVING TO DEBUG

Virtually all programmers seem to agree on this last recommendation: you need to get used to debugging[10]. "Learning how to debug is half of programming, so don't be discouraged" (Kim & Harnish, 2012). Once more, (Carver, 2013) provides great advice for beginners:

> "You think you've set up everything the way you're supposed to, you've checked and re-checked it, and it still. doesn't. work. You don't have a clue where to begin trying to fix it, and the error message (if you're lucky enough to have one at all) might as well say 'fuck you.' You might be tempted to give up at this point, thinking that you'll never figure it out, that you're not cut out for

---

[10] Debugging means identifying and removing errors from your programs.

this. […] It will happen to you as a beginner, but it will also happen to you as an experienced programmer. The main difference will be in how you respond to it"

Instead of getting frustrated with debugging, you should use it "as an essential part of the learning process" (Young, 2012). "Think of it as an opportunity to fix your misconceptions and improve your programming abilities" (Soare, 2015). In the end, spending time debugging is a normal part of web development – "get used to [it]" (Kim & Harnish, 2012).

Lastly, you can find two additional, large-scale collections of advice here (http://bit.ly/lrn-code-22) and here (http://bit.ly/lrn-code-23). The first resource is called "97 things every programmer should know" and has been curated by O'Reilly, one of the major publishers of programming books. It has collected "pearls of wisdom" from leading programming practitioners that offer various perspectives on all aspects of programming. The second resource is an exhaustive collection of "pragmatic software development tips" taken from the well-known "pragmatic programmer" book series – both are well worth checking out.

4. EVALUATION AND CRITICAL DISCUSSION OF FINDINGS

"Everybody in this country should learn to program a computer... because it teaches you how to think."

— **Steve Jobs**

As outlined in the introduction, entrepreneurs have neither time nor money – for this reason, this paper emphasizes making learning programming *efficient*. The goal is to be able to build a specific project as quickly as possible. While this approach is helpful in focusing the learning and avoiding wasting your time, it can be easy to forget that there is much more to computer science than just programming. "Coding is a start – a cool, fun, worthwhile and exciting means to get started with computing. But it should not be mistaken for the end. If the goal is to also [...] be better thinkers and problem-solvers, we need to broaden the scope of discourse from the narrow 'learn to code' view" (Grover, 2013).

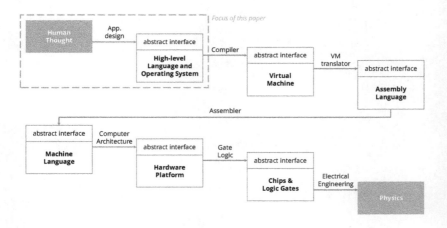

Figure 8: Levels of abstraction in computer science

Computer science has much more to it, as it offers to teach you what "a person should know to prosper in a computing-intensive world: the potential and the limits of computing devices, matching solutions to problems, and the ethics of information use" (Morris, 2003). Even though time might be limited, I strongly encourage readers to dig deeper than just learning programming for the web, and explore computer science and the surrounding community – which brought about fascinating innovations like open source or machine learning – as well. Good places to start are the "introduction to computer science" MOOCs by Stanford (http://bit.ly/lrn-code-24), MIT (http://bit.ly/lrn-code-25), or Harvard (http://bit.ly/lrn-code-26). Another interesting project worth checking out came out of the combined efforts of two Israeli universities and Google Research, and is called Nand2tetris. In it, you build a general-purpose computer system (including the hardware) from scratch, which shows you how all the different parts work together.

A second point that needs to be evaluated critically is the reliability of the sources used in this paper. Chapter 3 relies extensively on blog posts and other sources from the internet. It is clear that the internet contains unreliable sources, as anyone can publish there. Some people base their writing on barely more than their personal opinion, in what (Kinsella, 2016) calls "Tim Ferriss style non-rigorous scientific intuition" [11]. For this reason, I refrained from using anonymous sources like Reddit posts as a source. Instead, I only used contributions by either (i) programmers and instructors that are generally considered experts in their field, or (ii) self-learners who accomplished their goal of learning programming on their own by now being employed as software developers at known companies. Additionally, all 'hard' facts that are cited in this paper are exclusively taken from scholarly articles and published books.

---

[11] Tim Ferriss is an American author, entrepreneur, angel investor, and public speaker. His most famous book is titled the "4-hour workweek".

5. CONCLUSION AND RECOMMENDATIONS

"Desire is the key to motivation, but it's determination and commitment to an unrelenting pursuit of your goal – a commitment to excellence – that will enable you to attain the success you seek."

— Mario Gabriele Andretti

This thesis has been written to find the most efficient way of learning programming as a self-learner. In order to answer this research question, a comprehensive review of the existing literature has been carried out. Its results have been complemented with publicly published opinions of software developers, self-learners, and teachers of programming. The main findings of this paper are presented below in the form of actionable advice directly addressed to learners. They figure in their order of appearance throughout the paper, and are followed by suggestions for future research.

1. Establish a strong learning goal (3.1.1). A good example of such a goal would be a personal project you are motivated to build. Avoid jumping right into tutorials or MOOCs with the vague aspiration of "learning programming". Having a well-defined learning goal makes learning progress measurable, increases motivation and helps you persist when things get more complicated.

2. Gain an overview of the learning materials before you start (3.1.2). "Programming" is a broad term, which is why it is suggested that you narrow it down to web development as a beginner. Before starting to learn anything, you should get an overview of what the 'full stack' encompasses in order to be able to make an educated choice of language and technology.

3. Start with either JavaScript, Python, or Ruby as your first language (3.2.1). In general, there is no one "best" choice of a first programming language. The recommendation is based on the fact that all of the three suggested languages are commonly used in web development, have a promising outlook for the future, and are generally considered to be adapted for beginners by experts.

4. Establish a curriculum to guide your efforts, and use several resources in parallel (3.2.2). There is a staggering number of free high-quality resources available, and it is almost impossible to make sense of all of them in the beginning. For this reason, choose one or more curricula that will guide your learning. Additionally, there is no "one-stop shop" resource that will teach you everything – you can and should use several resources in parallel that will complement each other.

5. Optimize your learning by using techniques discovered by psychological research (3.3.1). The techniques introduced in this paper are easy to follow and implement. Make use of them and tailor them to your needs to improve your problem-solving abilities, your understanding of difficult concepts, your retention of new material, and to master procrastination.

6. Learn by doing: practice your programming skills and build real projects as soon as possible (3.3.2). Learning programming "is a hands-on effort; watching videos and solving multiple choice tests will not be sufficient" (Staubitz, Klement, Teusner, Renz, & Meinel, 2016). You should spend most of your time building projects.

7. Learn from advice by programmers, teachers, and other self-learners (3.3.3). The main advice you will find is that learning programming takes a long time, you should not be intimidated by 'genius programmers', and you should get used to debugging.

Lastly and perhaps most importantly, the main predictors of success when learning programming appear to be of *human* nature: motivation and persistence. Many beginners fall into the trap of worrying extensively about technical questions, such as which resource to choose, which language to pick, or which technology to use. This paper shows that as long as your choices remain within industry standards, they do not matter nearly as much as having a strong, overarching learning goal to stay motivated, and as being persistent by coding regularly.

Future research could tackle the apparent lack of research on self-learning programming. The quasi-totality of authors study university or high school students, and leave out self-learners. Additionally, many authors focus on technical aspects, i.e. on improving the interaction between students and the learning material (Thinakaran & Ali, 2016), and write for a target audience of teachers. Promising approaches that take into account human factors like motivation (Gomes & Mendes, 2007b) and that consider students' perspectives (Ateeq, Habib, Umer, & Rehman, 2014) are usually isolated and not holistic enough. A suggestion for future research might be to combine these more student-centered approaches with the large existing psychological research on leaning, and apply them to self-learning programming. Additionally, it could be of interest to see if the findings from studies on university students can be replicated in a self-learning environment. As the 'coding movement' has grown to be a veritable societal phenomenon, this direction of research seems promising and of relevance.

REFERENCES

In the references, you will find a list of resources mentioned in this paper, a table of figures, and the bibliography.

List of mentioned resources

Most resources mentioned in this paper can be found by simply googling their name. When this is not the case, I have included their URL in a shortened format (e.g. http://bit.ly/lrn-code-01) for better readability. The following table lists all 26 resources that were mentioned this way, including their 'original' link. They are listed in order of appearance.

Resource name	Shortened URL	Original URL
JavaScript is Sexy	http://bit.ly/lrn-code-01	http://javascriptissexy.com/how-to-learn-javascript-properly/
Odin Project Curriculum	http://bit.ly/lrn-code-02	http://www.theodinproject.com/courses
Lifehacker Python Curriculum	http://bit.ly/lrn-code-03	http://lifehacker.com/how-i-taught-myself-to-code-in-eight-weeks-511615189
Google's Guide to Technical Development	http://bit.ly/lrn-code-04	https://www.google.com/about/careers/students/guide-to-technical-development.html
Bachelor's Level CS Online Curriculum	http://bit.ly/lrn-code-05	http://blog.agupieware.com/2014/05/online-learning-bachelors-level.html
Zero to front-end hero – part 1	http://bit.ly/lrn-code-06	https://medium.freecodecamp.com/from-zero-to-front-end-hero-part-1-7d4f7f0bff02#.igwpy2dvr
Zero to front-end hero – part 2	http://bit.ly/lrn-code-07	https://medium.freecodecamp.com/from-zero-to-front-end-hero-part-2-adfa4824da9b#.742mvqfgf
'Awesome' list of online resources on GitHub	http://bit.ly/lrn-code-08	https://github.com/sindresorhus/awesome
Comprehensive list of MOOCs	http://bit.ly/lrn-code-09	https://www.class-central.com/courses/recent
Curated list of programming books #1	http://bit.ly/lrn-code-10	https://medium.mybridge.co/the-most-useful-free-ebooks-for-web-developers-3854767ee52f#.ccxntusvm

Curated list of programming books #2	http://bit.ly/lrn-code-11	http://www.linuxlinks.com/article/20150201134045961/BeginnerBooks.html
List of 500+ free programming books	http://bit.ly/lrn-code-12	https://github.com/vhf/free-programming-books/blob/master/free-programming-books.md
List of 33 curated YouTube channels	http://bit.ly/lrn-code-13	https://webuilddesign.com/33-useful-youtube-channels-for-learning-web-design-and-development/
Curated list of coding podcasts #1	http://bit.ly/lrn-code-14	https://medium.freecodecamp.com/the-best-podcasts-for-new-coders-and-the-best-tools-for-listening-to-them-df393b1c8dc#.p1m17owi1
Curated list of coding podcasts #2	http://bit.ly/lrn-code-15	https://sprint.ly/blog/developer-podcasts-of-hacker-news/
Curated list of coding podcasts #3	http://bit.ly/lrn-code-16	http://www.makeuseof.com/tag/15-top-notch-podcasts-programmers-software-developers/
Free Code Camp curriculum	http://bit.ly/lrn-code-17	https://www.freecodecamp.com/map
17 Coding Challenges from Codecondo	http://bit.ly/lrn-code-18	http://codecondo.com/coding-challenges/
Comprehensive list of programming problem sets on GitHub	http://bit.ly/lrn-code-19	https://github.com/vhf/free-programming-books/blob/master/problem-sets-competitive-programming.md
Automate the boring stuff	http://bit.ly/lrn-code-20	https://automatetheboringstuff.com/
Jennifer deWalt's 180 programming projects	http://bit.ly/lrn-code-21	https://jenniferdewalt.com/
97 programming tips by O'Reilly	http://bit.ly/lrn-code-22	http://programmer.97things.oreilly.com/wiki/index.php/Contributions_Appearing_in_the_Book
Pragmatic Programmer Tips	http://bit.ly/lrn-code-23	https://pragprog.com/the-pragmatic-programmer/extracts/tips
Stanford Computer Science 101 course	http://bit.ly/lrn-code-24	http://online.stanford.edu/course/computer-science-101-self-paced
MIT Introduction to Computer Science and Programming	http://bit.ly/lrn-code-25	https://www.edx.org/course/introduction-computer-science-mitx-6-00-1x-8
Harvard CS50: Introduction to Computer Science	http://bit.ly/lrn-code-26	https://www.edx.org/course/introduction-computer-science-harvardx-cs50x?gclid=CKDQ0JrA2c4CFViSvQod0RMMfA

Table of figures

Bibliography

Akiko, J. (2015, November 10). *What Nobody Tells You About Learning To Code—And Why That Makes It So Hard*. Retrieved from Free Code Camp Blog: https://medium.freecodecamp.com/what-nobody-tells-you-about-learning-to-code-and-why-that-makes-it-so-hard-22431ba27d78#.lfvja5hyc

Ali, A., & Mensch, S. (2008). Issues and challenges for selecting a programming language in a technology update course. *Proc. ISECON 2008* , (pp. 1-9).

Amer, H., & Ibrahim, W. (2014). Using the iPad as a pedagogical tool to enhance the learning experince for novice programing students. *2014 IEEE Global Engineering Education Conference (EDUCON)* (pp. 178-183). IEEE.

Andreessen, M. (2011, August 20). Why Software Is Eating The World. *The Wall Street Journal*, pp. 1-5.

Anewalt, K. (2008). Making CS0 fun: an active learning approach using toys, games and Alice. *Journal of Computing Sciences in Colleges, 23(3)*, 98-105.

Association for Computing Machinery (ACM). (2013). *Computer Science Curricula 2013: Curriculum Guidelines for Undergraduate Degree Programs in Computer Science*. IEEE.

Ateeq, M., Habib, H., Umer, A., & Rehman, M. U. (2014). C++ or Python? Which One to Begin with: A Learner's Perspective. *Teaching and Learning in Computing and Engineering (LaTiCE), 2014 International Conference*. IEEE.

Atwood, J. (2012, May 15). *Please Don't Learn to Code*. Retrieved from Coding Horror Blog: https://blog.codinghorror.com/please-dont-learn-to-code/

Atwood, J. (2013, March 22). *Why Ruby?* Retrieved from Coding Horror Blog: https://blog.codinghorror.com/why-ruby/

Baldwin, L. P., & Kuljis, J. (2001). Learning programming using program visualization techniques. *System Sciences, 2001. Proceedings of the 34th Annual Hawaii International Conference*. IEEE.

Barba, L. A. (2014, December 5). *Why I push for Python*. Retrieved from Lorena A. Barba Group Blog: http://lorenabarba.com/blog/why-i-push-for-python/

BBC. (2012, March 8). New York Mayor Michael Bloomberg takes coding course. *BBC News*.

Bergin, S., & Reilly, R. (2005a). Programming: factors that influence success. *ACM SIGCSE Bulletin 37(1)*, 411-415.

Bergin, S., & Reilly, R. (2005b). The influence of motivation and comfort-level on learning to program. *17th Workshop of the Psychology of Programming Interest Group, Sussex University* (pp. 293-304). Brighton, UK: PPIG.

Berglund, A., & Eckerdal, A. (2015). Learning practice and theory in programming education: Students' lived experience. *Proc. 3rd International Conference on Learning and Teaching in Computing and Engineering.* Los Alamitos, CA: IEEE Computer Society.

Bolhuis, S. (1996). Towards Active and Selfdirected Learning. Preparing for Lifelong Learning, with Reference to Dutch Secondary Education. *Annual Meeting of the American Educational Research Association.* New York, NY.

Boyes, K. (2003). *Creating an effective learning environment.* Moorabin, Vic.: Hawker Brownlow.

Boyle, R., Carter, J., & Clark, M. (2002). What makes them succeed? Entry, progression and graduation in Computer Science. *Journal of Further and Higher Education, 26(1),* 3-18.

Buck, J. (2011, September 20). *Four tips for learning how to program.* Retrieved from Signal v. Noise Blog: https://signalvnoise.com/posts/3014-four-tips-for-learning-how-to-program

Byrne, P., & Lyons, G. (2001). The effect of student attributes on success in programming. *ACM SIGCSE Bulletin, 33(3),* 49-52.

Cambridge University Press. (2011). *Cambridge Business English Dictionary.* Cambridge, UK: Cambridge University Press.

Capovilla, D., Berges, M., Mühling, A., & Hubwieser, P. (2015). Handling Heterogeneity in Programming Courses for Freshmen. *Learning and Teaching in Computing and Engineering (LaTiCE), 2015 International Conference* (pp. 197-203). IEEE.

Carey, B. (2014). *How we learn.* New York, NY: Random House.

Carter, J., & Jenkins, T. (2002). Gender differences in programming? *ACM SIGCSE Bulletin 34(3),* 188-192.

Carver, C. (2013, November 23). *Things I Wish Someone Had Told Me When I Was Learning How to Code.* Retrieved from Free Code Camp Blog: https://medium.freecodecamp.com/things-i-wish-someone-had-told-me-when-i-was-learning-how-to-code-565fc9dcb329#.wpd27p101

Chan, J. (2014, October 20). *How to become a self-taught developer: Q&A with Jon Chan, creator of Bento.io.* Retrieved from Learn to Code With Me: http://learntocodewith.me/posts/jon-chan-bento-io/

Chilana, P. K., Alcock, C., Dembla, S., Ho, A., Hurst, A., Armstrong, B., & Guo, P. J. (2015). Perceptions of non-CS majors in intro programming: The rise of the conversational programmer. *Symposium on Visual Languages and Human-Centric Computing (VL/HCC)* (pp. 251-259). IEEE.

Christensen, W. (2015, July 1). *How to Choose a Programming Language.* Retrieved from Treehouse Blog: http://blog.teamtreehouse.com/choose-programming-language

Cockburn, A. (2002). *Agile software development.* Boston, MA: Addison-Wesley.

Codementor. (2016a, January 6). *Why Learn JavaScript?* Retrieved from Best Programming Language for Me: http://www.bestprogramminglanguagefor.me/why-learn-javascript

Codementor. (2016b, February 19). *What Programming Language Should a Beginner Learn in 2016?* Retrieved from Codementor Insights: https://www.codementor.io/learn-programming/beginner-programming-language-job-salary-community

Codementor. (2016c, January 6). *Why Learn PHP?* Retrieved from Best Programming Language for Me: http://www.bestprogramminglanguagefor.me/why-learn-php

Combéfis, S., Beresnevicius, G., & Dagiene, V. (2016). Learning Programming through Games and Contests: Overview, Characterisation and Discussion. *Olympiads in Informatics, Vol. 10,* 39-60.

Dann, W. P., Cooper, S., & Pausch, R. (2011). *Learning to Program with Alice*. Upper Saddle River, NJ: Prentice Hall Press.

de Aquino Leal, A. V., & Ferreira, D. J. (2016). Learning Programming Patterns Using Games. *International Journal of Information and Communication Technology Education (IJICTE) 12(2)*, 34.

Dijkstra, E. W. (1989). On the cruelty of really teaching computing science. *Communications of the ACM, 32(12)*, 1398-1404.

Dreyfus, H. L., & Dreyfus, S. E. (1986). *Mind over machine: The power of human intuition and expertise in the era of the computer*. New York, NY: Free Press.

Eckerdal, A. (2009). Ways of thinking and practising in introductory programming. *Unpublished manuscript, Uppsala University, Sweden*, 1-29.

Elvers, G. C., Polzella, D. J., & Graetz, K. (2003). Procrastination in online courses: Performance and attitudinal differences. *Teaching of Psychology, 30(2)*, 159-162.

Ericsson, A. K., Krampe, R. T., & Tesch-Romer, C. (1993). The Role of Deliberate Practice in the Acquisition of Expert Performance. *Psychological Review, 100(3)*, 363-403.

Ericsson, A., & Pool, R. (2016, April 10). *Malcolm Gladwell got us wrong: Our research was key to the 10,000-hour rule, but here's what got oversimplified*. Retrieved from Salon: http://www.salon.com/2016/04/10/malcolm_gladwell_got_us_wrong_our_research_was_key_to_the_1000 0_hour_rule_but_heres_what_got_oversimplified/

Farag, B. (2016, May 10). Please don't learn to code. *TechCrunch*. Retrieved from TechCrunch.

Figg, T. E. (2013, January 13). *What language should I learn first?* Retrieved from Programming is Terrible Blog: http://programmingisterrible.com/post/40453884799/what-language-should-i-learn-first

Fincher, S., Robins, A., Baker, B., Box, I., Cutts, Q., de Raadt, M., . . . Petre, M. (2006). Predictors of success in a first programming course. *Proceedings of the 8th Australasian Conference on Computing Education* (pp. 189-196). Australian Computer Society, Inc.

Free Code Camp. (2016, August 1). *About*. Retrieved from Free Code Camp Website: https://www.freecodecamp.com/about

Fullstack Academy. (2016, August 1). *Why Fullstack JavaScript?* Retrieved from Fullstack Academy FAQ: http://www.fullstackacademy.com/faq

Garrison, D. R. (1997). Self-directed learning: Toward a comprehensive model. *Adult education quarterly, 48(1)*, 18-33.

Gentle, J. (2014, July 28). *What I tell all new programmers*. Retrieved from Seph Blog: https://josephg.com/blog/what-i-tell-all-new-programmers/

Gibbs, G., & Simpson, C. (2004). Conditions Under Which Assessment Supports Students' Learning. *Learning and Teaching in Higher Education 1(1)*, 3-31.

Gomes, A., & Mendes, A. J. (2007a). An environment to improve programming education. *Proceedings of the 2007 international conference on Computer systems and technologies* (p. 88). ACM.

Gomes, A., & Mendes, A. J. (2007b). Learning to program-difficulties and solutions. *International Conference on Engineering Education*. Coimbra, Portugal: ICEE.

Grover, S. (2013, June 2). *Learning to code isn't enough*. Retrieved from Stanford Graduate School of Education: https://ed.stanford.edu/news/learning-code-isnt-enough

Gugel, G. (2011). *2000 Methoden für Schule und Lehrebildung*. Weinheim, Germany: Beltz.

Guo, P. (2014, July 14). *Python is Now the Most Popular Introductory Teaching Language at Top U.S. Universities*. Retrieved from Communications of the ACM Blog: http://cacm.acm.org/blogs/blog-cacm/176450-python-is-now-the-most-popular-introductory-teaching-language-at-top-us-universities/fulltext

Guzdial, M. (2011, January 24). *Predictions on Future CS1 Languages*. Retrieved from Computing Education Blog: https://computinged.wordpress.com/2011/01/24/predictions-on-future-cs1-languages/

Hagan, D., & Markham, S. (2000). Does it help to have some programming experience before beginning a computing degree program? *ACM SIGCSE Bulletin, 32(3)*, 25-28.

Henry, A. (2014, July 2). *Productivity 101: A Primer to The Pomodoro Technique*. Retrieved from Lifehacker: http://lifehacker.com/productivity-101-a-primer-to-the-pomodoro-technique-1598992730

Herbert, C. (2007). *An introduction to programming with Alice*. Boston, MA: Course Technology.

Hilton, A. D. (2016, August 1). *Lecture 40 - Solving Programming Problems: A Seven Step Approach*. Retrieved from Programming and the Web for Beginners - Duke University: https://www.coursera.org/learn/duke-programming-web/lecture/Ao49s/solving-programming-problems-a-seven-step-approach

Hoffman, C. (2010, September 9). *A Command Line Primer for Beginners*. Retrieved from Lifehacker: http://lifehacker.com/5633909/who-needs-a-mouse-learn-to-use-the-command-line-for-almost-anything

Holvikivi, J. (2010). Conditions for successful learning of programming skills. In *Key competencies in the knowledge society* (pp. 155-164). Heidelberg, Germany: Springer.

Hu, M., Winikoff, M., & Cranefield, S. (2012). Teaching novice programming using goals and plans in a visual notation. *Proceedings of the Fourteenth Australasian Computing Education Conference* (pp. 43-52). Australian Computer Society, Inc.

JavaScript Scene. (2015, June 22). *Tech Survey Results*. Retrieved from Medium: https://medium.com/javascript-scene/javascript-scene-tech-survey-d2449a529ed#.8zv23d7sd

Jenkins, T. (2002). On the difficulty of learning to program. *Proceedings of the 3rd Annual Conference of the LTSN Centre for Information and Computer Sciences*, (pp. 53-58).

Kao, E. (2011). Exploring computational thinking at Google. *CSTA Voice, 7(2)*, 6.

Kaplan-Moss, J. (2015, April 12). *Keynote - Jacob Kaplan-Moss - Pycon 2015 [Video file]*. Retrieved from YouTube: https://www.youtube.com/watch?v=hIJdFxYlEKE&ab_channel=PyCon2015

Kelleher, C., & Pausch, R. (2005). Lowering the barriers to programming: A taxonomy of programming environments and languages for novice programmers. *ACM Computing Surveys (CSUR), 37(2)*, 83-137.

Khan Academy. (2016, August 1). *Intro to Algorithms*. Retrieved from Khan Academy Website: https://www.khanacademy.org/computing/computer-science/algorithms/intro-to-algorithms/v/what-are-algorithms

Kim, B., & Harnish, K. (2012). Geek Out: Adding Coding Skills to Your Professional Repertoire. *Charleston Conference Proceedings XXXII*, (pp. 448-452).

Kinnunen, P., McCartney, R., Murphy, L., & Thomas, L. (2007). Through the eyes of instructors: a phenomenographic investigation of student success. *Proceedings of the third international workshop on Computing education research*. ACM.

Kinsella, J. (2016, August 1). *Janki Method Refined*. Retrieved from Oxbridge Notes Blog: https://www.oxbridgenotes.com/articles/janki_method_refined

Krause, U. M., Stark, R., & Mandl, H. (2009). The effects of cooperative learning and feedback on e-learning in statistics. *Learning and Instruction, 19(2)*, 158-170.

Lahtinen, E., Ala-Mutka, K., & Järvinen, H.-M. (2005). A study of the difficulties of novice programmers. *ACM SIGCSE Bulletin 37(3)*, 14-18.

Larson, Q. (2016a, May 12). *Let's explore the universe of programming resources together.* Retrieved from Free Code Camp Blog: https://medium.freecodecamp.com/lets-explore-the-universe-of-programming-resources-together-77ff382a4c52#.yqc5ayz7s

Larson, Q. (2016b, March 4). *We asked 15,000 people who they are, and how they're learning to code.* Retrieved from Free Code Camp Blog: https://medium.freecodecamp.com/we-asked-15-000-people-who-they-are-and-how-theyre-learning-to-code-4104e29b2781#.xa7dzqebk

Larson, Q. (2016c, March 6). *Java, Ruby, and Go, Oh My!* Retrieved from Free Code Camp Blog: https://medium.freecodecamp.com/java-ruby-and-go-oh-my-6b5577ba2bc2#.v8v637gsv

Leacock, T. L., & Nesbit, J. C. (2007). A Framework for Evaluating the Quality of Multimedia Learning Resources. *Journal of Educational Technology & Society*, 44-59.

Leping, V., Lepp, M., Niitsoo, M., Tönisson, E., Vene, V., & Villems, A. (2009). Python prevails. *Proceedings of the International Conference on Computer Systems and Technologies and Workshop for PhD Students in Computing.* ACM.

Liew, Z. (2015, June 3). *An Overview of a Development Workflow.* Retrieved from Personal Blog: http://zellwk.com/blog/workflow-overview/

Long, J. (2012, September 25). *I Don't Speak Your Language: Frontend vs. Backend.* Retrieved from Treehouse Blog: http://blog.teamtreehouse.com/i-dont-speak-your-language-frontend-vs-backend

Lunden, I., & Shieber, J. (2016, July 12). *Codecademy, the free online coding school, raises another $30M led by Naspers.* Retrieved from TechCrunch: https://techcrunch.com/2016/07/12/codecademy-the-free-online-coding-school-raises-another-30m-led-by-naspers/

MacDonald, B. (2013, November 14). *Which Language Should You Learn First?* Retrieved from O'Reilly Radar: http://radar.oreilly.com/2013/11/which-language-should-you-learn-first.html

Mayer, R. E., Dyck, J. L., & Vilberg, W. (1986). Learning to program and learning to think: what's the connection? *Communications of the ACM, 29(7)*, 605-610.

Mayeux, S. (2016, May 2). *Learn to code like a Korean student learns English.* Retrieved from Free Code Camp Blog: https://medium.freecodecamp.com/what-i-learned-as-an-esl-teacher-will-help-you-learn-how-to-code-32a348afdd00#.6jg29ggod

McCartney, R., Eckerdal, A., Mostrom, J. E., Sanders, K., & Zander, C. (2007). Successful students' strategies for getting unstuck. *ACM SIGCSE Bulletin, 39(3)*, 156-160.

McCracken, M., Almstrum, V., Diaz, D., Guzdial, M., Hagan, D., Kolikant, Y. B.-D., . . . Wilusz, T. (2001). A multi-national, multi-institutional study of assessment of programming skills of first-year CS students. *ACM SIGCSE Bulletin, 33(4)*, 125-180.

McGill, T. J., & Volet, S. E. (1997). A conceptual framework for analyzing students' knowledge of programming. *Journal of research on Computing in Education, 29(3)*, 276-297.

McIver, L. (2000). The effect of programming language on error rates of novice programmers. *12th Annual Workshop of the Psychology of Programming Interest Group*, (pp. 181-192).

Michaelson, G. (2015). Teaching Programming with Computational and Informational Thinking. *Journal of Pedagogic Development, 5(1)*.

Miller, G. A. (1956). The Magical Number Seven, Plus or Minus Two: Some Limits on our Capacity for Processing Information. *Psychological Review, 63*, 81-97.

Morris, J. H. (2003, November 14). *Computer Science Is More Than Programming.* Retrieved from InformationWeek: http://www.informationweek.com/computer-science-is-more-than-programming/d/d-id/1021762?

Mullenweg, M. (2016, February 1). *Getting a Job After Coding Bootcamp.* Retrieved from Matt Mullenweg Blog: https://ma.tt/2016/02/getting-a-job-after-coding-bootcamp/

Norvig, P. (2001, January 2). *Teach Yourself Programming in Ten Years.* Retrieved from Peter Norvig Homepage: http://norvig.com/21-days.html

Oakley, B. (2014). *A mind for numbers.* New York, NY: Penguin Group.

Onah, D. F., Sinclair, J., & Boyatt, R. (2014). Dropout rates of massive open online courses: behavioural patterns. *EDULEARN14 Proceedings (2014),* (pp. 5825-5834).

Owens, K. (2013, August 19). *LoneStarRuby Conf 2013 - Hacking Passion by Katrina Owens [Video file].* Retrieved from YouTube: https://www.youtube.com/watch?v=rHLTltK1kss&feature=youtu.be&ab_channel=Confreaks

Pash, A. (2009, August 13). *How to Build a Web Application from Scratch with No Experience.* Retrieved from Lifehacker: http://lifehacker.com/5336113/how-to-build-a-web-application-from-scratch-with-no-experience

Pears, A., Seidmann, S., Malmi, L., Mannila, L., Adams, E., Bennedsen, J., . . . Paterson, J. (2007). A survey of literature on the teaching of introductory programming. *ACM SIGCSE Bulletin 39(4),* 204-223.

Pinola, M. (2013, May 12). *Which Programming Language Should I Learn First?* Retrieved from Lifehacker: http://lifehacker.com/which-programming-language-should-i-learn-first-1477153665

Porter, R., & Calder, P. (2004). Patterns in learning to program: an experiment? *Proceedings of the Sixth Australasian Conference on Computing Education-Volume 30* (pp. 241-246). Australian Computer Society, Inc.

Rist, R. S. (1995). Program structure and design. *Cognitive Science, 19(4),* 507-562.

Robins, A., Rountree, J., & Rountree, N. (2003). Learning and teaching programming: A review and discussion. *Computer science education, 13(2),* 137-172.

Rogerson, C., & Elsje, S. (2010). The Fear Factor: How It Affects Students Learning to Program in a Tertiary Environment . *Journal of Information Technology Education,* 147-171.

Sievers, D. (2013, January 6). *Memorizing a programming language using spaced repetition software.* Retrieved from Derek Sievers Blog: https://sivers.org/srs

Soare, A. (2015, June 11). *8 barriers to overcome when learning to code.* Retrieved from The Next Web: http://thenextweb.com/dd/2015/06/11/8-barriers-to-overcome-when-learning-to-code/

Soloway, E., & Spohrer, J. C. (1989). *Studying the novice programmer.* Hillsdale, NJ: Lawrence Erlbaum.

Song, L., & Hill, J. R. (2007). A conceptual model for understanding self-directed learning in online environments. *Journal of Interactive Online Learning, 6(1),* 27-42.

Sonmez, J. (2011, January 8). *Solving Problems, Breaking it Down.* Retrieved from Simple Programmer: https://simpleprogrammer.com/2011/01/08/solving-problems-breaking-it-down/

Sourour, B. (2016, June 21). *The Practical Guide to Becoming a Professional Web Developer.* Retrieved from Free Code Camp Blog: https://medium.freecodecamp.com/the-practical-guide-to-becoming-a-professional-web-developer-2f255bc25c90#.8g6kipist

Spiegel, D. (2016, June 8). Uber's books still top secret, but its biggest weakness isn't. *CNBC.*

Spolsky, J. (2005, January 2). *Advice for Computer Science College Students.* Retrieved from Joel on Software Blog: http://www.joelonsoftware.com/articles/CollegeAdvice.html

Stack Overflow. (2016, March 17). *2016 Developer Survey.* Retrieved from Stack Overflow: http://stackoverflow.com/research/developer-survey-2016

Staubitz, T., Klement, H., Teusner, R., Renz, J., & Meinel, C. (2016). CodeOcean??? A versatile platform for practical programming excercises in online environments. *2016 IEEE Global Engineering Education Conference (EDUCON)* (pp. 314-323). IEEE.

Stern, W. [. (2016, August 4). *2016/2017 MUST-KNOW WEB DEVELOPMENT TECH - Watch this if you want to be a web developer [Video file].* Retrieved from YouTube: https://www.youtube.com/watch?v=sBzRwzY7G-k&ab_channel=LearnCode.academy

Surprenant, A. M., & Neath, I. (2013). *Principles of memory.* Psychology Press.

Tanzer, D. (2012, November 28). *Deliberate Practice is Overrated.* Retrieved from David Tanzer Blog: http://www.davidtanzer.net/deliberate_practice

The Odin Project. (2016, August 1). *Introduction to Web Development.* Retrieved from The Odin Project Homepage: http://www.theodinproject.com/introduction-to-web-development

The Odin Project. (2016, August 1). *This is Your Path to Learning Web Development.* Retrieved from The Odin Project Homepage: http://www.theodinproject.com/courses

Thinakaran, R., & Ali, R. (2016). An Empirical Study: Learning Programming Using eLearning. In *Envisioning the Future of Online Learning* (pp. 125-132). Singapore: Springer.

Thornton, J. (2014, August 29). *Medium's CSS is actually pretty f***ing good.* Retrieved from Medium: https://medium.com/@fat/mediums-css-is-actually-pretty-fucking-good-b8e2a6c78b06#.gaaaff3qh

Trautman, E. (2015a, February 26). *The Beginner's Dilemma: Your First 100 Hours of Code.* Retrieved from Viking Code School Blog: https://www.vikingcodeschool.com/posts/the-beginner-s-dilemma-your-first-100-hours-of-code

Trautman, E. (2015b, February 4). *Why Learning to Code is So Damn Hard.* Retrieved from Viking Code School Blog: https://www.vikingcodeschool.com/posts/why-learning-to-code-is-so-damn-hard

Verdú, E., Regueras, L. M., Verdú, M. J., Leal, J. P., de Castro, J. P., & Queirós, R. (2012). A distributed system for learning programming on-line. *Computers & Education, 58(1)*, 1-10.

Vivian, R., Falkner, K., & Szabo, C. (2014). Can everybody learn to code? Computer science community perceptions about learning the fundamentals of programming. *Proceedings of the 14th Koli Calling International Conference on Computing Education Research* (pp. 41-50). Koli: ACM.

Weimer, M. (2014, May 14). *Is Rereading the Material a Good Study Strategy?* Retrieved from Faculty Focus Blog: http://www.facultyfocus.com/articles/teaching-professor-blog/rereading-material-good-study-strategy/

White, J. Z. (2016, May 17). *From Zero to Front-end Hero (Part 1).* Retrieved from Free Code Camp Blog: https://medium.freecodecamp.com/from-zero-to-front-end-hero-part-1-7d4f7f0bff02#.k7c0p5g5j

Wikipedia. (2016a, August 1). *Autodidacticism.* Retrieved from Wikipedia: https://en.wikipedia.org/wiki/Autodidacticism

Wikipedia. (2016b, August 1). *Web development.* Retrieved from Wikipedia: https://en.wikipedia.org/wiki/Web_development

Wikipedia. (2016c, August 1). *Front-end web development.* Retrieved from Wikipedia: https://en.wikipedia.org/wiki/Front-end_web_development

Wikipedia. (2016d, August 1). *Problem solving.* Retrieved from Wikipedia: https://en.wikipedia.org/wiki/Problem_solving

Wikipedia. (2016e, August 1). *Spaced repetition.* Retrieved from Wikipedia: https://en.wikipedia.org/wiki/Spaced_repetition

Wikipedia. (2016f, August 1). *Spacing effect.* Retrieved from Wikipedia: https://en.wikipedia.org/wiki/Spacing_effect

Wikipedia. (2016g, August 1). *Algorithm*. Retrieved from Wikipedia: https://en.wikipedia.org/wiki/Algorithm

Williams, A. (2015, October 1). *Coding Bootcamp vs Self-Study*. Retrieved from Course Report: https://www.coursereport.com/blog/bootcamp-vs-self-study-the-complete-guide

Wilson, B. C., & Shrock, S. (2001). Contributing to success in an introductory computer science course: a study of twelve factors. *ACM SIGCSE Bulletin, 33(1)*, 184-188.

Wing, J. M. (2006). Computational thinking. *Communications of the ACM, 49(3)*, 33-35.

Winslow, L. E. (1996). Programming pedagogy—a psychological overview. *ACM SIGCSE Bulletin, 28(3)*, 17-22.

Wolf, G. (2008, April 21). *Want to remember everything you'll ever learn? Surrender to this algorithm*. Retrieved from Wired: http://www.wired.com/2008/04/ff-wozniak/

Wozniak, P. (1999, February 1). *Effective learning: Twenty rules of formulating knowledge*. Retrieved from Supermemo Blog: https://www.supermemo.com/en/articles/20rules

Wranx. (2016, April 26). *Ebbinghaus and the forgetting curve*. Retrieved from Wranx Blog: http://www.wranx.com/ebbinghaus-and-the-forgetting-curve/

Yadin, A. (2011). Reducing the dropout rate in an introductory programming course. *ACM Inroads*, 71-76.

Young, S. H. (2012, September 9). *The Beginner's Guide to Learning to Program*. Retrieved from Scott H. Young Blog: https://www.scotthyoung.com/blog/2012/09/09/learn-to-program/

Zendler, A. (2015). Computer science education teaching methods: An overview of the literature. *International Journal of Research Studies in Computing, 4(2)*, 3-11.

Zhang, W. Y., & Perris, K. (2004). Researching the efficacy of online learning: A collaborative effort amongst scholars in Asian open universities. *Open Learning, 19(3)*, 247-264.